The Thought
of
Their Heart

The Thought of Their Heart

by

Solange Hertz

TUMBLAR HOUSE

'Bona Tempora Volvant'

Arcadia
MMXV

Printed in the United States of America

ISBN 978-0-9883537-7-0

Visit our website at www.tumblarhouse.com

For us in the field ...

A generation ago, when these little effusions on Sacred Heart devotion and the Holy Rosary were first published as "the extraordinary devotion God provided against our extraordinary times" and "the ultimate liturgy," already Church and world were in turmoil. Since then the agony has mounted without let, for in progress is a decisive battle which can only intensify until it is finally over.

In the spiritual warfare engulfing us, Sr. Lucy of Fatima told Fr. Fuentes in the famous conversation she had with him in 1957 that,

> We should not wait for an appeal to the world from Rome on the part of the Holy Father ... nor wait for the call to penance to come from our bishops in our diocese, nor from the religious congregations. No! ... It is necessary for each one of us to reform himself spiritually. Each person must not only save his own soul, but also all the souls that God has placed in his path.

For this combat heaven taught the Church Militant some very special maneuvers which must not be foolishly abandoned after what have proved to be only preliminary skirmishes. The hour has come to perform them in earnest, perfecting them by ever more arduous practice, with increasing confidence, for victory is certain for those who master them.

As a humble reminder to those bedraggled foot soldiers straining doggedly in the ranks or holed up in dugouts as the case may be, *The Thought of His Heart* and *The Holy Rosary* are herein offered once again, newly edited and joined under the title *The Thought of Their Heart*. For good measure the little piece "Mary's Remnant" which first appeared in the November 30, 1990 issue of *The Remnant* has been added.

Solange Hertz
Feast of St. Longinus, 1994

Table of Contents

I. HEART TROUBLE

It's hard to love. These days it doesn't seem to come naturally anymore—if it ever did. As our Lord warned us, towards the end evil would be so rampant charity would grow cold.

More or less we have all become spiritual cardiacs, our every move conditioned by the dread possibility of imminent heart failure. Loving in the face of the malice confronting us at every turn is such uphill work, so great a strain, only the force of a divine command driving us from behind could keep us at it. Reason alone would tell us to relax. Lots of us have, and that hasn't helped our environment.

"Hear, O Israel: the Lord our God is one Lord. Thou shalt love the Lord thy God with thy whole heart, and with thy whole soul, and with thy whole strength" *(Deut. 6:4-5)*.

To refuse to love is to disobey God. *Thou shalt love*, or else. The crisis of faith in our thinking today manifests itself as a crisis of love in our wills. Not believing, we can't love; not loving, we stop believing. All God's lesser prescriptions depend on His command to love. To disobey it disqualifies us for all other tests, whereas obeying it automatically leads us to do everything God wants us to do, and to avoid everything He doesn't want us to do. It eliminates all quibbling, dispels all minor confusions and hesitations. It makes life rough, but exceedingly meaningful.

The vast majority of us give up. "For the Lord tries you, that it may appear whether you love him with all your heart, and with all your soul—or not" *(Deut. 13:3)*. For those who don't give up, suddenly everything is relevant. If we persist, we find boredom is a luxury we can't afford. There isn't time.

Whoever says loving is easy either lies or hasn't tried it, or both. It's the most difficult achievement that man in his fallen state could possibly tackle, yet his life depends on it. It's so difficult God himself had to come down eventually and show us how, because we hadn't the heart for it. As things developed, He had to give us that too. And that wasn't easy for Him either.

If loving is hard, allowing himself to be loved seems to be even harder for modern man. He finds it almost impossible to believe he is loved, that anybody really wants him. This requires faith, he discovers. His receiving mechanisms are so deranged he cannot humbly and gratefully accept the free gift of love even when it is offered. Psychiatrists' offices are filled with people who sincerely feel themselves so rejected—even when they are not—they can no longer function as healthy human beings.

Who can blame them? From the cradle we're told we're a nuisance, some of us by our very mothers, who look upon our birth as little more than an obstacle to self-fulfillment in a brave new world. Others have fathers who resent having to support them. Nursery schools and academia are thronged with young outcasts.

Even so, these are the lucky ones, created through the happy conjunction of sperm and ova aggressive enough to have successfully run the gauntlet of contraceptive traps, slaps, loops, jellies, misinformation and propaganda. Somehow they were spared the ministrations of assorted vasectomists, abortionists, zero population planners, programmed gynecologists, and fetal researchers who had (like God) only one message to deliver, but in reverse: "We don't want you. Maybe a few selected others, but not *you*."

They are quite specific in any given case. It's personal, and we take it personally. Not only we don't want you, we are told, but ideally, we don't want you even to *be*, not for one moment. Abortions are messy. Contraception is the real answer, because we don't want you to have life at all. WE HATE YOU! And we hate irresponsible people who clutter the world with you.

As we know, by now millions of us are gifted only briefly with life. Discarded as embryos in the laboratory, perhaps in the course of experimentation, we never get so far as a bassinette, to be hated there by those who should love us. We are dismembered in the womb, cradled piecemeal in a rolling garbage can by hands which will only rock the world. Who reaches maturity must face other tests. They must survive child engineering of all descriptions, perverted history texts and scientism, impure sex education, volleys of adult literature and art, mutilated worship—and already, in dark corners, sterilization of the unfit and euthanasia, all implemented by the technological craft harnessed to the goals of the concentration camp.

That our neighbor doesn't love us is only too evident in the vast majority of our human encounters, but this is the lesser blow to our hearts. There are crazed philosophers and divines who labor to acquaint us with what, down deep, we are bitterly tempted to suspect: that God doesn't want us either. Could a God who loves us make us live in such a world? He must hate us!

That's silly, they tell us. How could God hate you? God is dead! Whether He loves us or not is academic, because He doesn't exist, and never did. He was invented by us, you idiots. He is us. Why don't you grow up and admit it? Be mature. Stand on your own feet for a change.

Only God could help at a time like this. Only He can tell us He is alive and loves us, because at this point in history we don't dare believe anyone else. We have been so fed on lies, so betrayed by those responsible for us, no one less than God could restore our faith, not only in Him but in ourselves. Our trust in man is gone. The credibility gap devours everything he tells us. He's too treacherous, too unreliable. We're exhorted on all sides to "open ourselves to one another in mutual trust," but we who have been betrayed know better. We are "closed" and wary. We wouldn't trust our own grandmothers, in some cases with very good reason.

Well, let's not feel guilty about it. While on earth, God himself reached the same conclusion, and said so to his disciples:

Beware of men, for they will deliver you up in councils (parish? national? ecumenical?), and they will scourge you in their synagogues ... Brother shall deliver brother to death, and the father the son: and the children shall rise up against their parents and shall put them to death *(Matt 10:17,21)*.

Like us, God has been rejected. When He was born as man there was no room for Him at the inn in Bethlehem, and in His maturity He was snubbed in His own temple in Jerusalem, eventually put to death outside its walls. Before that had come a time when He could no longer walk openly among His own people *(John 11:54)*. Often He had to hide, as He does even now. He "wouldn't trust himself to them, because he knew what was in man" *(John 2:23-25)*. He told us plainly, "One is good: God" *(Matt. 19:17)*.

In the final analysis the only man who can be trusted is in fact God, and He must be trusted and believed in utterly. "You believe in God, believe also in me ... And where I go you know, and the way you know" *(John 14:1,4)*. "Follow me!" *(Matt. 16:24)*.

Patiently He explained the outrageous task that lay before us, how all the while never trusting man, we must nevertheless love him—to the point of laying down our life for him. All the while being wise as serpents, we must be innocent as doves, prepared to forgive him seventy times seven times for what he does to us, will continue to do to us, and will do to us ever more viciously the more perfectly we follow Christ. What's hard about liking people who like us? As He himself noted, that's easy.

"Thou shalt love the Lord thy God with thy whole heart and with thy whole soul and with thy whole mind. This is the greatest and the first commandment. And the second is like to this: Thou shalt love thy neighbor as thyself," as well as you can.

Or, as W.H. Auden put it, you shall love your crooked neighbor with your crooked heart. Whether we like it or not, "On these two commandments depend the whole law and the prophets" *(Matt. 22:37-40)*. Luckily, love isn't a function of the feelings, for God never commands the impossible. Love is an operation of the will, directed by the intellect. The feelings can go along or not as they please. If they do, so much the better; if not, too bad for them, not us. Wanting to love, doing the works of love is to love.

In order to show us exactly how this is done in real life, God led us personally, step by step, from Bethlehem to Egypt to Nazareth, to Calvary and to heaven. "Learn of Me," He said, "because I am meek and humble of heart" *(Matt. 11:29)*. "As I have loved you, you also love one another" *(John 13:34)*.

This, knowing what we do about Calvary and all that led up to it, is preposterous! Especially for people with heart conditions! You'd have to have the heart of God to do that sort of thing, *really* to do it.

And that's the heart of the matter.

That's why He promised us centuries ago through His prophet Ezechiel that in the last days He would replace our calcified hearts with a heart of flesh in order to love so impossibly. He knew we didn't have the heart for it, that we would have to have a brand new one:

"And I will give you a new heart, and put a new spirit within you: and I will take away the stony heart out of your flesh, and will give you a heart of flesh" *(Ez.36:26)*.

Ezechiel couldn't have known what we know now, that the heart of flesh God intended to give us was nothing less than His own. With God's heart in our breasts we can love as God loves, and do His will.

II. HAVING A HEART

Earthbound logic would expect the divine heart to be a purely spiritual one, proper to a God who is purely spirit. But that's only logical, and underestimates God's power and generosity. Incredible as it seems, when God gave us His heart, He gave us a human one. We were given the heart of Jesus, our Savior, the Father's only-begotten Son. In order to confer it on us, this Son became man.

Saints and mystics throughout the ages have maintained that this would have happened even if we had never sinned and Christ need never have died for us, for God had determined from all eternity to seal and crown His creation with nothing less than himself. Intending by the Incarnation not merely our salvation, but primarily our incorporation into His divinity, He wished to invest us with all His goods and His very life. "Is it not written in your law," Jesus asked the Jews, "'I said you are gods'?" *(John 10:35)*.

Because we were created with a natural attraction or appetite for God, we can love Him easily enough from the outside, as it were, with our natural faculties. As Voltaire put it, if there were no God, we would have to invent one, so programmed are we to complete ourselves in something other and greater, outside ourselves. Idolatry is a standing temptation for creatures like us, made for love and little else.

The gods of secularism today are legion. There's plenty to choose from, but so great is our natural hunger for God, that for want of the truth, we've lately taken to lumping together the two greatest Commandments by worshipping one another! Call it world brotherhood, Communism, secular humanism or whatever you like, it is an attempt to find God at eye level and stop there, loving Him from outside in creatures.

It's possible, after all, to go through the motions of a Christian life by our own unaided strength, putting on a show good enough to fool a lot of the people a lot of the time, but way down deep, at gut level, we aren't doing anything out of the ordinary. Pagans can do that, for ethical behavior is not holiness. Most any well-intentioned person is capable of it, given sufficient approbation from his peers. But sooner or later we give ourselves away. In depth, the performance isn't authentic.

To love God and our neighbor as we are meant to, we must love from *inside God*, as the Persons of the Blessed Trinity love one another. To do this it's obvious that something completely beyond natural human endowments must be added to us. We have to get inside God, not only to love others as He loves them, but even more important, to love God as He loves himself, in the Godhead. His "new commandment" is to love as He loves. Faithful to His own substantial order, He loves us as He loves himself. We must therefore continue to love our neighbor as ourselves, but *in Him*.

This is what Baptism makes possible. By joining us sacramentally to the second Person of the Blessed Trinity, we are introduced into the company of the Father and the Holy Ghost, with whom He is one, and ever familiar. When John and Andrew first met Jesus and asked Him where He lived, He answered simply, "Come and see" *(John 1:39)*. They could hardly have known when they accepted this invitation that He meant to take them all the way home with Him, to meet the Family we call the Most Blessed Trinity. Yet this is eventually what He did, and intends to do for anyone who visits Him.

Really to love, in spirit and in truth, we must become divine, because God is love. There is no love but God. Any other love is mere natural appetite.

This is very mysterious, because the heart of Jesus is not only human in the psychological sense, but truly one of flesh, just as God promised Ezechiel. Like any heart, it is a physical, pulsating, blood-pumping muscular valve located within the chest cavity, not immediately visible to the naked eye, but absolutely essential to the life of the whole body. Even the brain depends on it. Those who fix "clinical" death to the moment the brain ceases emitting waves have decided for reasons of their own to ignore the fact that the heart can continue pumping without the help of the brain, whereas the brain can't function an instant without the support of the heart. Who needs a course in anatomy to know that? Or to know that by divine decree Jesus even now depends on His heart for resurrected physical life just as we do on ours?

The bald carnal facts on which devotion to the Sacred Heart of Jesus rests have constituted from the beginning a nagging obstacle to its propagation in some quarters. For such, to adore a bodily organ, even one belonging directly to God, is repugnant. It's a hard saying, of a piece with our Lord's instruction to eat His Body and drink His Blood, which turned away many of His followers even in His own day. Pope Pius XII took cognizance of their difficulties in his incomparable encyclical on the Sacred Heart, *Haurietis aquas*, without minimizing them.

There will always be those who cannot endure stubborn mystery. They will if possible reduce it to ambiguity, because ambiguity can be lived with on the natural plane. It adapts to circumstances, meaning whatever they want it to mean at any given moment. As in the new Mass the Most Precious Blood of Christ is reduced to "spiritual drink" and His Body to a "symbol of community," so may the Sacred Heart be reduced to some super-Valentine. Throughout history heretics have found the Incarnation itself shocking, too "material," in fact, rather gross. Lucifer may have been the first. According to the Fathers the occasion of his revolt was precisely that God neglected to become an angel, preferring to unite His divinity to a lowly nature half composed of crass matter.

Tertullian stood at the height of orthodoxy when he said that the flesh is "the hinge of salvation." All the Sacraments depend on it. We have to accept it and cope with it. Pope Pius XII stated flatly that "the whole validity of the physical Heart of Jesus as a natural symbol of the Person of the Word rests on the fundamental truth of the hypostatic union." Take it—or leave it and deny the Incarnation. It should suffice to say that God's grace builds on nature, finding in it a compatible tool for spiritual works. The physical heart of Jesus is therefore a most proper starting point for personal union with His divinity, for with this Heart, He loves us. What follows, follows.

To say the Heart of God is a physical organ is plain truth; to say it is only that is rankest falsehood. For one thing, its sense element provides symbol, which human psychology needs and craves in order to express what cannot be entirely expressed in words. These last reflect well enough ideas created by the mind, but can go no further than that. Religious use of symbols comes closest to conveying transcendent, unutterable reality.

So understood, the heart isn't merely the engine of physical activity, but the very principle of our spiritual acts. Scripture doesn't hesitate to ascribe thinking to the heart. Mary "pondered in her heart" *(Luke 2:19)*. Our Lord asked the disciples walking to Emmaus why "thoughts arose in their hearts" *(Luke 24:38)*. The heart makes decisions: When Moses "was full forty years old it came into his heart to visit his brethren" *(Acts 7:23)*. St. Peter, exposing Ananias' fraud, asks him, "Why have you conceived this thing in your heart?" *(Acts 5:4)*.

Hearts may be veiled, blind to the truth *(2 Cor. 3:15)*, or they may be hard, obstinate, proud, avaricious, hostile. They are also characterized as credulous or incredulous: "O foolish and slow of heart to believe all things which the prophets have spoken!" complained our Lord *(Luke 24:25)*. Hearts are also described as sorrowful. St. Paul, like the ancient prophets, designates the heart as the object of true circumcision *(Rom. 2:28)*. There is no human act or emotion which can't be ascribed to the heart, for it is the compendium of human personality, the very seat and source of moral life.

"A good man out of the good treasure of his heart brings forth that which is good," said our Lord. "And an evil man out of the evil treasure brings forth that which is evil. For out of the abundance of the heart the mouth speaks" *(Luke 6:45)*. "For from the heart come forth evil thoughts, murders, adulteries, fornications, thefts, false testimonies, blasphemies" *(Matt. 15:19)*. "Whoever shall look on a woman to lust after her has already committed adultery with her in his heart" *(Matt.5:29)*.

Our Lord proposed the heart as the center and citadel of the inner man as opposed to the outer—on which the fate of the outer ultimately depends. Common speech testifies that what a man is "at heart" is what he really is, all appearances to the contrary notwithstanding. Our Lord quoted Isaiah to the Pharisees, saying, "This people honors me with their lips, but their heart is far from me" *(Matt. 15:8)*, and He told them how useless it is to scour the outside of the cup when the inside was "full of rapine and iniquity" *(Luke 11:39)*. To the pure of heart He promised nothing less than the vision of God.

The human heart is a mystery, "perverse above all things, and unsearchable. Who can know it?" The Creator alone, who "has searched out the deep," can understand it. "I am the Lord who search the heart and prove the reins!" *(Jer. 17:9-10; Ecclus. 42:18)*.

To dismiss it as the source of all bodily and spiritual acts is still too easy. The concept of "heart" is much richer than that. It embodies rather that indefinable, elusive *mélange* of corporal and spiritual in us which renders our acts specifically human, neither entirely animal, nor entirely spiritual. It is the mixing chamber, as it were, where matter and spirit—those two apparently irreconcilable opposites—are united in proper amounts under compression to produce the life we call "human." When sin enters our lives, it is admitted there.

Of all human hearts the Heart of Jesus is Most Sacred. Sin excepted, what is true of all is true of His to a super-eminent degree, for it is the material instrument not just of His holy Humanity, but of His divinity. It is the "organ of the Trinity," as

St. Mechtilde and St. Gertrude so happily put it. It is the very nexus, or mixing chamber, of the Incarnation. In the heart of Jesus not only do matter and spirit join, but God and man, divinity and humanity.

What God has joined together, let no man put asunder! In Christ we are wed to God indissolubly, eternally, for better or for worse.

Our Lord no longer suffers, and His heart is no longer subject to the vicissitudes of earthly life, but it still exists in glory, actually functioning as the indispensable organ of His Mystical Body, pumping the life-giving Precious Blood into every member. Whoever would live with God's life, and love with God's love, must accept the Sacred Heart as his own. There is no other way.

III. CHANGE OF HEART

St. John the Evangelist told St. Gertrude that divine wisdom was reserving the full revelation of the Sacred Heart for the last days, when it would be most desperately needed, when, as our Lord foretold, "many shall be scandalized and shall betray one another and shall hate one another."

She asked St. John:

> Wherefore, then have you kept such absolute silence about this, that you have never written anything, however little it might be, that would make it understood, at least for the profit of our souls?

He answered:

> My mission was to deliver to the Church, in her first age, a simple word on the uncreated Word of God the Father, that would suffice until the end of the world to satisfy the understanding of the whole human race, yet without any person ever succeeding in fully understanding it. But to tell the sweetness of these pulsations has been *reserved for the present time*, so that in hearing of these things the world that is growing old and whose love is weakening may be revived.

We would have to deny the evidence of our senses not to see that our world has grown even older since St. Gertrude's time and may in fact now be near its natural end. Those who interpret the present confusion as sign of "renewal" may be mistaking the erratic sputters of a guttering flame for blazing glory: "Nation shall rise against nation, and kingdom against kingdom; and there shall be pestilences and famines and earthquakes in places ... and many false prophets shall arise and seduce many ... Take heed that no man seduce you!" *(Matt. 24, passim.)*

Only God is to be trusted.

If these days are actually upon us, it could be significant that we have also entered the age of heart transplants, a thing unheard of until now. Of all the portents of the space age agony, this may turn out to have the richest prophetical meaning. In its desperate attempts to confer abundance of life on man by purely material means, modern science is in fact effecting a parody of the divine dispensation. What signs and wonders may it yet produce whereby to deceive the elect!

The idea of living with another person's heart is something we are only just beginning to think about in physical terms. New hearts for old? Like it or not, the thing is being done, and like artificial insemination, the homicidal methods so far developed to effect the transfer render the practice grievously sinful. Moral theologians are only beginning to study all its consequences and ramifications. (Let them read Ezechiel.)

What we read about being perpetrated on lowly matter on operating tables is a pale shadow—perhaps a diabolic mirror image—of a divine operation God planned from the outset, but meant to occur in spirit and in truth. It's clear that from earliest times God told us He intended to replace our sin-damaged hearts with that of His beloved Son:

"And I will give them a new heart to know me, that I am the Lord: and they shall be my people, and I will be their God: because they shall return to me with their whole heart" *(Jer.24:7)*.

Long before He was conceived in the immaculate womb of the Virgin Mary the prophets had begun to describe and acquaint us with the heart of the Messiah which was to be ours, loving, suffering, yet always generous, glorious and totally innocent:

> Their leader shall be of themselves," says Jeremiah, "and their prince shall come forth from the midst of them. And I will bring him near, and he shall come to me: for who is this that sets his heart to approach me, says the Lord? *(Jer. 30:21)*.

The Psalms reveal Him as one who, like us, wants to be loved. He is shown complaining, "My heart has expected reproach and misery. I looked for one that would grieve together with me, but there was none: and for one that would comfort me, and I found none." On the contrary, "they gave me gall for my food: and in my thirst they gave me vinegar to drink" *(Ps.68:21-22)*, because this is what we can expect from mere men. "My heart is become like wax melting in the midst of my bowels" *(Ps.21:15)*.

Yet, "In the head of the book it is written of me that I should do thy will: O my God, I have desired it, and thy law in the midst of my heart" *(Ps.39-9)*. "Therefore my heart has been glad, and my tongue has rejoiced: moreover my flesh also shall rest in hope" *(Ps.15:9)*. "Thou has proved my heart and visited it by night, thou has tried me by fire: and iniquity has not been found in me" *(Ps.16:3)*.

That God, utterly holy, wants to love and be loved is what He has been telling us from the beginning. It is the substratum of every message He has ever delivered to us. To resist His love is, quite simply: hell. Damnation is the state of those who will not love, nor allow themselves to be loved. To preserve us from this fate He became visible for us, so His divine personality might become dear to us in human dress.

"Who sees me, sees the Father," He told Philip. And, "He that believes in me, does not believe in me, but in him that sent me. And he that sees me, sees him that sent me" *(John 12:44-45)*. To hear God speak we have only to listen to our Lord: "For I have not spoken of myself: but the Father who sent me commanded what I should say, and what I should speak. And I know that his commandment is life everlasting. The things therefore that I speak, even as the Father said unto me, so do I speak" *(John 12:44-50)*.

To know what God is really like we have only to read the Gospels. There His Heart can be read like a book. "Learn of me, because I am meek and humble of heart" He tells us *(Matt. 11:29)*, patiently explaining that to live God's life we must first find out what He's like. We can't love what we don't know.

And in the Gospels we discover He's all heart. Our Lord admitted publicly that He hadn't come to judge the world—which properly speaking is a function of the intellect, an operation of truth. That would inevitably come later. First He came to save the world, which is a function of the will, a work of love. This is hardly surprising, because God, who is Truth, is also love *(John 14:6; 1 John 4:8)*. Rejecting God's love is to sever us from His truth, for they are one.

At the stage of disintegration our civilization has reached today, it may be that only love can reach us. Our poor brains, saturated with error, and bewildered by trying to untangle the moral chaos soliciting our judgment at every turn, have little strength left for theology or the mental disciplines making use of mere logic and reason. We are desperate, and crave the immediate support only love can give. Although love depends on knowledge, love carries further, and knowledge not ordered to love is fruitless anyway. Even devils believe.

Perhaps we should be using that hallowed word charity rather than love, for we are not speaking here of the "love" of pentecostalism or related heresies so rampant today which presume to fly above doctrinal difficulties as if they were of no real importance. Love divorced from truth is not charity; it isn't even real love, but mere affection. If rejecting God's love severs us from His truth, then rejecting His truth equally severs us from His love for, as we noted, they are one.

In our present predicament, however, there may not be much time left for speculation. With the accelerated tempos goading us, we may well thank God for the stark succinctness of the

Gospels, set before us even more starkly by Holy Mother Church in her dogmatic definitions. The truth is out for anyone who really wants it. Leisure for argument is past. Will we love God, or not?

"You are my friends," He told us, "if you do the things that I command you ... Abide in my love" *(John 15:14,9)*. To love someone is to want to know everything about him, and to do everything we can to please him. To love someone is to identify with him as closely as possible. And how is it possible not to identify with someone who wants to be loved? Don't we all?

"Let this mind be in you which was also in Christ Jesus ... for it is God who works in you, both to will and to accomplish, according to his good will" *(Phil. 2:5,13)*.

"Can you drink the chalice that I shall drink?" God asks us, as He asked St. Peter and the sons of Zebedee *(Matt. 20:22)*. "Will you lay down your life for me?" *(John 13:38)*.

Do we have the heart to? Do we have the heart not to, considering that He did it first for us, even when we were sinners?

There is a story that St. Lutgard once petitioned our Lord for some special insights into the Psalms. He granted her request, but soon she realized that all this extraordinary information was distracting her prayer more than helping it, and she began fretting.

"Well, then, what *do* you want?" our Lord asked her. "Lord," she finally told Him, I want your *Heart*."

To which Jesus replied, "I want *your* heart."

So they traded hearts.

Thus began a long tradition. In classical spiritual parlance such exchanges came to be referred to as "mystical marriage," or "transforming union," bespeaking the perfect union of wills which marks the summit of a life of prayer. The tragedy is that it occurs only rarely in great saints, and not in everyone of us, as God intends it should:

> Cast away from you all your transgressions, by which you have transgressed, and make to yourselves a new heart, and a new spirit: and why will you die, O Israel? ... And I will give you a new

heart, and put a new spirit within you: and I will take away the stony heart out of your flesh, and will give you a heart of flesh. And I will put my spirit in the midst of you: and I will cause you to walk in my commandments, and to keep my judgments, and do them ... And you shall remember your wicked ways, and your doings that were not good: and your iniquities, and your wicked deeds shall displease you *(Ezech.18:31; 36:26-27,31)*.

Living by the heart of God, we should be able to say with St. Paul, "I live, now not I, but Christ lives in me," heart to heart, "who loved me and delivered himself for me *(Gal. 2:20)*.

A change of heart is the only remedy for what the sin of Adam did to us. It heals our corrupted power of loving.

IV. FROM THE BOTTOM OF THE HEART

Modern devotion to the Sacred Heart of Jesus didn't begin in a convent, as many suppose. It began on Calvary, at the foot of the Cross. It was there that St. John saw, in physical terms, that God is love. He tells us how it happened, at the moment the Roman soldiers arrived to break the legs of the three crucified that good Friday so they could be dispatched quickly and taken down before the start of the onrushing Jewish festivities:

"But after they were come to Jesus, when they saw that he was already dead, they did not break his legs." Nevertheless, to make sure He was dead, "one of the soldiers with a spear opened his side: and immediately there came out blood and water." Lest there be any doubt of what he saw, St. John adds, "He that saw it gave testimony: and his testimony is true. And he knows that he says true: that you also may believe" *(John 19:33-5)*.

This duty was properly accorded to the beloved disciple, who next to the Immaculate Mary was closest to the Heart of Jesus, on which he had rested at the Last Supper. St. Paulinus of Nola says, "John, who rested blissfully on the breast of our Lord, was inebriated with the Holy Ghost; from the Heart of the all-creating Wisdom he quaffed an understanding which transcends that of any creature" *(Epistola, 21)*.

St. John, the first apostle of devotion to the Sacred Heart, hadn't set down his account from motives of personal piety. By divine inspiration he wrote it in his old age, after years of meditation after the event, for the whole world to read and absorb. He was aware that "these things were done that the scripture might be fulfilled," for the prophet Zachary had long ago predicted that "they shall look on him whom they have pierced" *(John 19:33-37)*.

Modern medical science would seem to bear out St. John's testimony of water as well as blood issuing from the Sacred

Heart, a fact he found so significant. Dr. Pierre Barbet, basing his conclusions on his own professional experience of dead bodies and the evidence of the Holy Shroud of Turin, has this to say in *A Doctor Looks at Calvary*:

> The lance must have entered above the sixth rib, have perforated the fifth intercostal space and penetrated deeply beyond it. With what would it then have met? The pleura and the lung. If St. John's soldier had given the blow with his lance in an almost vertical direction, he would, first of all, have scarcely been able to perforate the intercostal space; if he had, the point of his lance would have become lost in the lung, in which he would only have been able to draw blood from a few pulmonary veins. He might have caused a great deal of blood to flow, but no water. The pleural fluid, if there was any, would have necessarily been accumulated *at the base of the pleural cavity*, which was behind and *below* the level of the wound. What I have in mind, as will be understood, is hydrothorax or dropsy of the chest, the pleural fluid which would be transuded as the result of the death agony, which we shall find in the pericardium ...
>
> The blow with the lance was then oblique and not far off the horizontal, which is easy to understand if the cross, as I think, was not very high ... And then: the point moved naturally across the thin, forward part of the right lung and, according to the radiographs, after a course about three inches in length, reached the right border of the heart enveloped in the pericardium. Now ... the part of the heart which extends to the right of the breastbone is the right auricle. And this auricle, which is prolonged upwards by the superior *vena cava*, is in a corpse always filled with liquid blood.

It is the bottom of the heart.

Dr. Barbet concludes that after our Lord's exceptionally painful death agony, caused by the terrible cramping of crucifixion, the pericardial fluid would have been exceptionally abundant. St. John, the eye-witness, would have seen it flowing from the pericardium at the same time that the blood flowed from the right auricle of the heart.

> He would have imagined that the serum was water, for it has that appearance. As there was no other water in the body other than

the serous fluid, it could not have been pure water. We ourselves use the word hydropericardium, which means the water contained in the pericardium.

These physical facts must be insisted on, for they are of major importance, as St. John was the first to realize. The mystery of the Incarnation and Death of our Lord is no disembodied doctrine preaching flight from the body into pain-free, bloodless nirvana. As he stressed in his second Epistle, "For many seducers are gone out into the world, who confess not that Jesus Christ is come in the flesh: this is a seducer and an antichrist" *(2 John, 7)*.

The blood and water gushing from the heart of Christ after He was already dead was gratuitous beyond all thinking. What more of himself beyond His life was there to give? St. Catherine of Siena, who like St. Lutgard had exchanged hearts with our Lord, wondered at this. "Sweet, spotless Lamb," she exclaimed to Him, "you were dead when your side was opened! Why, then, did you will that your Heart should be thus wounded and opened by force?"

Replied our Lord:

> For several reasons of which I will tell you the principal. My desires regarding the human race were infinite, and the actual time of suffering and torture was at an end. Since my love is infinite, I could not therefore by this suffering manifest to you how much I loved you. That is why I willed to reveal to you the secret of the Heart by letting you see it open, that you might well understand that it loved you far more than I could prove to you by a suffering that was over.

This outpouring was the headwaters of a wealth of grace destined to flow forever over creation from the depths of the Sacred Heart. He himself foretold it, as St. John also recorded.

At the last day of the feast of Tabernacles before His Passion He had shouted to the entire crowd of worshippers, "If any man thirst, let him come to me; and let him drink who believes in me. As the scripture says: Out of his belly shall flow rivers of living water!" And St. John explains, "Now this he said of the Spirit which they should receive who believed in him" *(John 7:37-39)*.

This living water, the supernatural life of grace, is the same He had already promised to the Samaritan woman, soon to be flooding visibly from its source on the Cross. Centuries before that the prophets Isaiah, Ezechiel and Zachary had said that we would "draw waters with joy out of the Savior's fountains," hardly aware that they would spring from the body of a man who was God. *(Is. 12:3)*.

"In that day," promised Zachary, "there shall be a fountain open to the house of David, and to the inhabitants of Jerusalem: for the washing of the sinner, and of the unclean woman" *(Zach. 13:1)*. And lest there be any doubt left, St. Paul tells us that the rock which Moses struck in the desert from which water gushed for the people was in fact Christ *(1 Cor. 10:4)*.

As the Litany says, the Heart of Jesus is truly the gate of heaven, the house of God, a burning furnace of love, abyss of all virtues, fountain of life and holiness, the propitiation for our sins and the delight of all the saints, the Heart in whom are all the treasures of wisdom and knowledge which God would ever give to man. Dogmatically and historically, the early Fathers saw the Church herself proceeding in the form of blood and water from the transfixed Heart, recognizing her as the second Eve issuing from the opened side of Christ as the first Eve had originally been taken from the side of Adam. Tertullian says:

> If Adam was a type of Christ, then the sleep of Adam was a type of the sleep of Christ, who slept in death, in order that through a similar cleaving of the side the true mother of the living might be formed, namely the Church *(De Anima, 43)*.

The Church, almost an incarnation of the Holy Ghost, is Christ's supreme gift among us. Through her and her Sacraments His love is poured over the world. As St. Thomas teaches:

From the side of Christ there flowed water for washing and blood for redeeming. And so the blood that flowed is associated with the Sacrament of the Eucharist, and the water with the Sacrament of Baptism. Baptism however has its power to make clean from the efficacy of the Blood of Christ.

To refuse the Church is therefore to refuse our Lord's ultimate bequest to us. This means we reject Him, for to refuse a gift is to refuse its giver. St. Irenaeus, after St. Polycarp the direct disciple of St. John, went so far as to say that the living water Christ dispenses through His Church is not merely grace, but the Holy Ghost himself, the very Gift of the Father:

The Church is the fountain of the living water that flows to us from the Heart of Christ. Where the Church is, there is the Spirit of God, and where the Spirit of God, there is the Church and all grace. But the Spirit is truth. He who has no part in this Spirit will receive no nourishment or life at the breast of our mother Church, nor can he drink of the crystal-clear spring which issues from the Body of Christ *(Adversus Haereses: 24,1)*.

There is no true devotion to the Sacred Heart apart from devotion to His Church. It is the devotion of the Church, for she is His Mystical Body. The Sacred Heart is her heart.

V. CUT TO THE HEART

Heartless as we are, it's only too easy to feel resentment against God. Down here dodging the common cold, pollution, in-laws, mental disease, taxes and nuclear fission, it takes some doing to love a God who is supremely happy, ineffably pure and always in control of everything. Blind envy alone drives us to hate Him.

If we worship Him, as often as not it's only because we're afraid of what will happen to us if we don't. That He loves us we can believe on a beautiful spring day, disporting ourselves on the Italian Riviera on an expense account, but how to believe it when we're starving in Biafra, maimed in a blitz or screaming with AIDS or terminal cancer?

Looking at what he saw around him—and in him—Schopenhauer came to the conclusion that the world was in fact created by a malevolent being who delighted in seeing people suffer. He poisoned modern philosophy with categorical pessimism, paving the way for Nietzsche and the atheistic humanism which is becoming our world religion. Is it any wonder that today so many blaspheme, proclaiming that God, thank God, is dead? All that remains now is to prove it by trying to live without Him, so we can really believe it.

This means we have to get that Man off the crucifix. Does religion have to be so gruesome?

"Let Christ the king of Israel come down now from the cross, that we may see and believe!" *(Mark 15:32).* Unbelievers began shouting this on Calvary, and they're getting louder all the time. Today they tell us that venerating the Cross is like venerating an electric chair. And so it is, and God did die on it.

Had God remained aloof from us, pure Spirit, beyond pain, with power of life or death over us, those of us who could find the courage might defy Him as one defies a particularly outrageous bully. The ulcerated Job on his dunghill in fact asked Him why He didn't pick on someone His size. How can God stoop to punishing a creature so helpless against Him as man is? The Book of Job is witness to the unavoidable presence of this gnawing question in the minds of the parties to the old Covenant—now usually referred to as "the problem of innocent suffering." Subjectively it more often poses itself as, "How can we get back at Him?"

If God hadn't become man, we could never love Him, that is, not really. In our miserable little way, we might feel superior, the way a skinny kid can go down beaten, bloody, but morally victorious in a hopeless fight with the neighborhood Goliath. When God ascended the Cross, however, He demolished all our pretenses. "Emptying himself" of all His divine prerogatives in order to meet us on our ground, He let us do whatever we wanted to Him. Who can glory over such humility?

From every crucifix He pleads, "Look, look, I suffer, like you, even more than you. I have a body like yours, a soul like yours. I'm hated like you. Don't *you* hate Me! *Please love me.* Don't you see how much I love you?"

To love someone is to give him an awesome power to hurt us. It's to hand him a knife. By taking on our flesh God made himself vulnerable to us in this way, soliciting our love. And we struck Him—to the very heart—with Longinus' spear, even after He was already dead. We wanted to make sure, with officious excess.

The heart of flesh which Christ offers us is therefore not intact. It is *wounded*. If His divine Heart is a symbol, its wound is more poignantly so. What the Heart is unable to convey of itself, the wound proclaims all too plainly. The wound renders visible the invisible hurt we deal Him daily with such deadly intent. There is now no way of concealing it. The blow to the Heart wasn't a wound like those to the hands or the feet. It was interior, mortal, delivered to the depths of the divine Being, aimed at the Holy of Holies of the Godhead.

Exclaims Christ in the ancient liturgy for Good Friday:

> O My people, what wrong have I done you? When have I ever grieved you? Answer Me! ... What more should I have done for you that I have not done? I planted you to be My very own and

most choice vine, but you have borne Me bitter fruit: for with vinegar you have quenched My thirst, and with a spear you have pierced your Savior's side.

O, holy God!
O, holy, mighty God!
O, holy, immortal God, have mercy on us!
"Indeed this man was the son of God!" *(Mk.15:39)* said the centurion whose duty it was to administer the blow. It couldn't have been anyone else. No one has ever loved us like that, and no one ever will.

Longinus was the first convert to what we call today Devotion to the Sacred Heart of Jesus, the first member of the Apostleship of Prayer. With his spear he tore open for succeeding generations all the riches of God. As holy Mass tells us, through this mystery of water and blood, we have become partakers of His divinity, who has deigned to become partaker of our humanity, Jesus Christ our Lord.

For those who see and accept this truth, God is no longer merely the omnipotent Creator who has to be reckoned with whether we like it or not. He is someone with whom we can enter into intimate personal relations, with all the give and take of joy and suffering which a love affair demands. And no one can be forced into a love affair.

Accepting the invitation has been the work of saints throughout the ages. The first recorded vision of the Sacred Heart as such is the aforementioned one granted to St. Lutgard in the 13th century, but the devotion itself was well developed long before that. Beginning with St. John the Apostle, patristic theologians like Origen, St. Augustine, St. Hippolytus, St. Justin Martyr and St. Cyprian established it on firm doctrinal ground. As early as the third century, meditation on the piercing of

Christ's side was a regular practice for devout Christians every afternoon at three o'clock.

The middle ages, during which the great mystics flourished, evidenced particularly intense cultivation of prayer to the Sacred Heart: St. Anselm of Canterbury, St. Bernard of Clairvaux, St. Francis of Assisi, St. Mechtilde, St. Angela of Foligno, St. Margaret of Cortona, St. Bonaventure, St. Catherine of Siena and St. Albert the Great are some of the spiritual giants who have left testimony to the power and vitality communicated to them from the divine Heart.

Voluminous literature on the subject was bequeathed us by St. Gertrude the Great, the Benedictine mystic of Helfta who, as we have seen, was granted a special revelation from St. John. Writing under obedience her famous *Book of Extraordinary Grace*, she revealed the exchange of her heart for our Lord's, as had happened with St. Lutgard and later with St. Catherine and many others. In her own talented and charming way, she tells us our Lord said He gave it to her,

> ...that it may accomplish all that you cannot accomplish yourself, and thus all will seem perfect in you to My eyes; for even as a faithful servant is always ready to execute the commands of his master, so from henceforth My Heart will be always ready at any moment to repair your defects and negligences.

St. Gertrude thought this was really too much. She,

> ...wondered and feared ... but the Lord consoled and encouraged her by this comparison: "If you have a beautiful and melodious voice, and take much pleasure in chanting, will you not feel displeased if another person, whose voice is harsh and unpleasant, and who can scarcely utter a correct sound, wishes to sing instead of you, and insists on doing so?"

On one occasion when St. Gertrude was too ill to attend a sermon she wanted to hear, our Lord appeared suddenly and offered to preach one to her himself. It was on the Sacred Heart. Inasmuch as she kindly set it down for us, we can do no less than reproduce it here:

Beginning by making her recline on His Heart "so that her soul touched it," and she could feel two wonderful movements within it, our Lord explained:

> Each of these movements operates the salvation of man in three different manners. The first [movement] operates the salvation of sinners: the second, that of the just. By the first [manner] I converse continually with My eternal Father—I appease His anger against sinners, and I incline Him to show them mercy. By the second, I speak to My saints, excusing sinners to them and urging them with the zeal and fidelity of a brother to intercede with God for them. By the third [manner], I speak to sinners themselves, calling them mercifully to penance, and awaiting their conversion with ineffable desire.
>
> By the second movement of My Heart, I [first] invite My Father to rejoice with Me for having poured forth My precious Blood so efficaciously for the just, in whose merits I find so many delights. Secondly, I invite all the heavenly host to praise My providences, that they may return Me thanks for all the benefits I have granted to them, and that I may grant them more in the future. Thirdly, I speak to the just, giving them many salutary caresses, and warning them to profit faithfully by them from day to day and hour to hour. As the pulsations of the human heart are not interrupted by seeing, hearing, or any manual occupation, but always continue without relaxation, so the care of the government of heaven and earth and the whole universe cannot diminish or interrupt for a moment these two movements of My divine Heart which will continue to the end of ages.

Our Lord's sermon, we note, was the soul of brevity. He later told his congregation of one that,

> Henceforth I shall use your heart as a canal through which I will pour forth the impetuous torrents of my mercy and consolation which flow from My loving Heart on all those who shall dispose themselves to receive it by having recourse to you with humility and confidence.

Thus does intimacy with our Lord inevitably lead us to make a return to Him by embarking on an apostolate to others.

According to the Roman Martyrology, St. Longinus was in due course beheaded for the faith in Cappadocia.

VI. THE OPEN HEART

The history of devotion to the Sacred Heart is in a very real sense a gradual revelation of the secret life of the Church. Its prologue, written in the heart of St. John as he reclined against the Lord's breast at the Last Supper, broadcasts its first rhythms to the world, setting the tempo for the dramatic rending on Calvary.

Veneration for the wound inflicted there seems to have been the initial form of the cult among the faithful. From this wound, the "door in the ark," there gradually issued the proliferation of grace we now know as Sacred Heart devotion, ramifying and increasing through time, space and circumstance to fit all the needs and conditions of worshippers truly seeking intimacy with their Lord. It elicited tears of repentance, prompted praise, encouraged confident petition and proffered earth's reparation to heaven for its sins against Love.

For centuries the movement developed quietly in the privacy of religious houses and the souls of gifted individuals until it permeated the whole Church in ranks both clerical and lay. In addition to the saints already mentioned, among its devotees must be numbered St. Anselm, St. Frances of Rome, St. Lawrence Justinian, St. Bernardine of Siena, St. Joan of Valois, St. Peter of Alcantara, St. Fidelis of Sigmaringen, St. Antoninus, St. Peter Canisius, St. Francis de Sales—to list but a few of those canonized. Others who spread its benefits are legion. Carthusians, Franciscans, Benedictines, Dominicans, each produced its particular "school" of spirituality based on affection for the wounded Heart of the Savior.

The wealth of art, literature, and liturgy both canonical and popular which has come down to us on the subject attests to its vigor and sanctifying power. Already in the middle ages the "Little Hours of the Glorious Heart of Jesus Christ" were recited in Cologne. A Feast of the Holy Lance was approved by Pope Innocent VI for the second Friday after Easter. By the fifteenth century a proper Feast of the Sacred Heart was observed by the Dominicans of Alsace. Very early there had appeared pictorial representations of the Sacred Heart almost identical to the one with which we are now all familiar, among them a beautiful woodcut by Lucas Cranach. Without multiplying data, suffice it to emphasize that there is nothing new, or even peculiar to any one century, about devotion to the Sacred Heart. Like all dogma it develops, not through change, but through organic revelation, as an acorn can be seen to become an oak, or a child a man.

Not surprisingly, it was St. John Eudes, the apostle of the Immaculate Heart of Mary, who was instrumental in directing modern piety towards the Heart of her Son. Called by Pope St. Pius X "initiator, teacher and apostle of the liturgical cult of the Sacred Heart," he had begun by drawing heavily on the writings of the old Cologne Carthusians so as to establish the cult on solid theological ground. By 1672 he had succeeded in obtaining ecclesiastical approval for a Mass of the Sacred Heart to be celebrated in the communities of his own Order, the Congregation of Jesus and Mary.

The very next year, on the feast of St. John the Apostle, December 27, 1673, the torrents of private revelations converged explosively in the Visitation convent at Paray-le-Monial in France. It was there that our Lord, appearing to the humble young nun, St. Margaret Mary Alacoque, chose to set the seal of divine approval on what had until then been a most salutary practice in the Church, but which nevertheless remained a private affair—a kind of "inside track" for fleeter spirits.

Our Lord had once told St. Gertrude:

> Whenever you desire to obtain anything from Me, offer Me My Heart, which I have so often given you as a token of our mutual friendship, in union with the love which made Me become man for the salvation of men; and I give you this special mark of

friendship, that this shall be presented to whomsoever you pray for, as a rich man would present a coffer to his friend to supply himself therefrom with all he needed.

After four great apparitions in Paray from 1673 to 1675, our Lord's "mark of friendship" was no longer "special." Destined for the public domain, devotion to the Sacred Heart was soon to be enjoined upon all. If we are to believe the words of St. John the Apostle and the ancient prophets concerning the Heart of God, we who are living three hundred years later must be about to witness nothing less than the last moments of the world.

"In the latter days you shall understand these things," promised Jeremiah. "The THOUGHTS of HIS HEART to all generations: to deliver their souls from death and feed them in famine" (*Introit*, Mass of the Sacred Heart).

Recapitulating the experience of generations of saints and mystics, St. Margaret Mary herself relates the extraordinary occurrences:

> One day as I was praying before the Most Holy Sacrament and had a little more leisure than usual—normally the tasks I was given did not leave me much time—I was completely invested with the divine presence, so completely that I utterly forgot myself and where I was. I surrendered myself to this divine spirit and abandoned himself to the force of His love. He made me lean for a long time on His divine breast, while He revealed to me the marvels of His love and the inexplicable secrets of His Sacred Heart, things which He had hitherto always hidden from me and now disclosed for the first time. But He did it in so plain and effective a manner as to leave me no room for doubting it, such were the results that this grace produced in me, who am always afraid of deceiving myself with regard to what I assert to take place within me.
>
> He said to me: "My divine Heart is so inflamed with love for men, and for you in particular, that it can no longer contain within itself the flames of its ardent love, and must needs spread them by your means, and manifest itself to men and enrich them with the precious treasures that I will reveal to you. These treasures contain the graces of salvation and sanctification necessary to draw men out of the abyss of unworthiness and ignorance, for the

accomplishment of this great design, in order that all may be done by Me."

Then He asked for my heart, which I implored Him to take, and having done so, He placed it within His adorable Heart, showing it to me as a little atom being consumed in a glowing furnace; and then withdrawing it thence like a burning flame in the shape of a heart, He replaced it whence He had taken it, saying: "Behold, my beloved, a precious pledge of My love, which is inserting in your side a tiny spark of its most fiery flames, to serve as your heart and to consume you until your last moment. And as a sign that the great favor I have done you is not imaginary, but the foundation of all those that I still have to bestow upon you, although I have closed the wound in your side, the pain of it shall ever remain with you; and though hitherto you have adopted the name of my slave, I now give you that of the beloved disciple of My Sacred Heart."

The following year:

This divine Heart was shown me on a throne of flames; it was more resplendent than the sun and transparent as crystal; it had its own adorable wound, and was surrounded by a crown of thorns, signifying the stings caused by our sins, and there was a Cross above it, implying that from the first moment of the Incarnation the Cross was planted in it.

... He showed me that the ardent desire that He had of being loved by men and of rescuing them from the path of perdition, where Satan brings them in crowds, had made Him form the design of manifesting His Heart to them, with all the treasures of love, of mercy, of graces, of sanctification and salvation which it contains, in order that He might enrich all who were willing to render it and procure for it, all the love, honor and glory in their power, with the profusion of these divine treasures of the Heart of a God from which they spring. He told me that this Heart was to be honored under the form of a heart of flesh, the picture of which He wished to be exposed and worn by me on my heart, in order to impress its love upon my heart, and fill it with all the gifts with which His Heart is full, and so destroy all irregular movements within it.

He said that wherever this holy picture should be exposed to be honored, He would lavish His graces and blessings, and that this blessing was a last effort of His love to favor men in these latter times with a most loving redemption, to deliver them from the thralldom of Satan, which he intended to overthrow, that He might place us under the gentle liberty of the dominion of His love, which He wished to reestablish in the hearts of all those willing to practice this devotion.

There was a third vision that same year:

On one occasion while the Blessed Sacrament was exposed, I felt wholly drawn within myself by an extraordinary recollection of all my senses and powers. Jesus Christ, my gentle Master, presented himself to me, all resplendent with glory, His five wounds shining like so many suns. From His Sacred Humanity issued flames on all sides, especially from His adorable breast, which resembled a furnace, and which was open, disclosing to me His most loving and lovable Heart, the living source of these flames. It was then that He discovered to me the unspeakable wonders of His pure love, and to what an excess He had gone in loving men, from whom He received only ingratitude and neglect, "which I feel much more," He said, "than all I suffered in My Passion. If only they made me some return for My love, I should think but little of all that I have done for them and should wish, if it were possible, to do yet more. But they have only coldness and rebuffs to give Me in return for all My eagerness to do them good. Do you at least give Me consolation by making up for their ingratitude as far as you are able."

"In the first place you will receive Me in the Blessed Sacrament as often as obedience will allow you, no matter what mortifications and humiliations may result to you, but they must be regarded as pledges of My love. Moreover you will receive Holy Communion on the first Friday of each month, and every Thursday night I will make you share the heavy sorrow that it was my will to feel in the Garden of Olives. This sadness will bring you, without your comprehension, to a state of agony harder to bear than death. In order to be with Me in that humble prayer which I then offered to My Father in the midst of My agony, you will rise between eleven o'clock and midnight, so as to lie prostrate with me for an hour, with your face to the ground, both to appease God's anger and to ask mercy for sinners."

The last and greatest revelation took place during the octave of Corpus Christi, 1675:

> As I prayed before the Blessed Sacrament ... I received from my God excessive tokens of His love, and felt myself desirous to make some return and to render Him love for love. Then He said to me, "You cannot make Me any better return than by doing what I have so often asked of you."

> Then revealing His divine Heart, He said: "Behold this Heart which has so loved man that it has spared nothing, even to exhausting and consuming itself, in order to give them proof of its love, and in return I receive from the greater number nothing but ingratitude, contempt, irreverence, sacrilege and coldness in this sacrament of My love. But what I feel still more is that there are hearts consecrated to Me who use Me thus. Therefore I ask of you that the first Friday after the octave of the Blessed Sacrament shall be kept as a special feast in honor of My Heart, to make reparation for all the indignities offered to it, and as a Communion day, in order to atone for the unworthy treatment it has received when exposed upon the altars. I also promise that My heart shall shed in abundance the influence of its divine love on all those who shall thus honor it or cause it to be so honored."

Propagated tirelessly through the efforts of St. Margaret Mary, her director Bl. Claude de la Colombière and other dedicated members of the Order of the Visitation and the Society of Jesus—to whom this work of mercy was specially entrusted—devotion to the Sacred Heart spread like wildfire, eventually receiving the enthusiastic approbation and support of ecclesiastical authority.

"I am come to cast fire on the earth," our Lord told His disciples, "and what will I, but that it be kindled!" *(Luke 12:49)*.

Private piety, without losing anything of its character, became official. In 1856 Pius IX extended to the whole world a Feast of the Sacred Heart, already approved in 1765 by Clement XIII. In conjunction with the Encyclical *Annum Sacrum*, Leo

XIII consecrated the world to the divine Heart in 1899. In 1928 Pius XI raised the Feast to the highest liturgical rank, with Mass and Office for an entire octave, bringing out at the same time the encyclical *Miserentissimus Redemptor*.

Hundreds of confraternities and many new religious orders, not to mention the Apostleship of Prayer, had arisen and prospered with papal approval, promoting the devotion until now, when not to have heard of the Sacred Heart or First Fridays is hardly to be a Catholic. In 1956 Pope Pius XII crowned the devotion with the magnificent encyclical *Haurietis aquas*, in its way a veritable little summa of "the thought of His Heart," which Jeremiah promised would be best understood in the latter days.

What is expected of us now?

VII. TAKING HEART

That our Lord expects us to reciprocate His advances goes without saying. The Heart St. Margaret Mary was shown was not only wounded, it was blazing. Such love demands return.

But how is this possible? With the best will in the world, with the "continual sacrifice" failing perceptibly around us as the prophet Daniel prophesied, what chance is there to comply with our Lord's requests? How can First Friday devotion, so inextricably bound to the Real Presence, flourish in desecrated churches and decimated parishes where even the divinity of Christ can be denied with impunity? Even the Feast of the Sacred Heart has been moved to a day other than that specified by our Lord! Mustn't we acknowledge that in due time Sacred Heart devotion must disappear along with private Confession, Latin, Benediction, Gregorian chant, novenas, Litanies, Stations of the Cross, vestments, statues and all the rest?

No. Desirable and efficacious as they are, pious practices are fortunately not the essence of the dedication our Lord wants. "All must be fully persuaded," says Pope Pius XII, "that in our worship of the August Heart of Jesus the external practices of piety are not the most important thing. Nor should we see the chief reason for this worship in the blessings which Christ our Lord promised in private revelations."

These promised blessings are considerable. In a famous letter to Fr. Croiset, St. Margaret Mary said of those promoting the devotion that our Lord,

> ...will make their salvation sure, He will not allow anyone consecrated to Him to be lost. He has a great desire to be known, loved and honored by His creatures. In this way He can satisfy to some extent the ardent desire to spread His love. He will shower graces upon them for their salvation and sanctification. He will be their sure refuge at the hour of death. He will take them under His protection and defend them from their enemies. To obtain all this,

of course, they must lead lives in conformity with His divine maxims.

Such blessings, the Pope reminds us, "were promised precisely in order that men might fulfill more fervently the principal duties of the Catholic religion, that is, *love* and *expiation*, to the more effective enrichment of their own spiritual life." In fact, he continues, "So much value must be given to devotion to the Sacred Heart that it shall be regarded in practice as the most accomplished way of professing the Christian religion" *(Haurietis aquas)*.

Official approval in no way derogates from its personal, voluntary character. Although it is offered to all, it is offered to all individually, as a very special, infallibly efficacious spirituality. It is an invitation to intimacy which does not oblige in the same way, surely, that faith obliges. It remains a means, but as Pius XII points out, it is an *extraordinary* means given to believing Catholics, one which each neglects at his peril in these extraordinary times—times to which it is proportioned.

Through the divine mercy, it can be ours when all other means might fail. Its significance increases daily with the growing failure of the priesthood and the progressive mutilation of the Sacraments. In circumstances where the Church herself seems to be fading from sight and it looks as if every man must fend for himself, devotion to the Sacred Heart may be a last resort for him who "understands these things."

Its power lies in its peculiarly personal character. There is no way for organized secularism to get at it. It's not a love affair between God and the aggregate "humanity" we hear about ad nauseam these days. It isn't even an affair between God and the People of God. It's an affair between Jesus Christ and me, Person to person, One to one, with all the impossible demands and exigencies, delights, obligations, impositions, frustrations and consummations such a friendship brings in its wake. As a matter of fact, the whole thing is incredible to anything less than brilliant faith. It is the divine hand of friendship personally extended to us against the dehumanizing desperation of the computer age. Suddenly, no Social Security number is required, no records searched, because everything is out in the open between us.

If nothing else, the experience will be humbling. This isn't the "cosmic Christ" of de Chardin awaiting us perfunctorily at the end of the evolutionary process. Nor is it the vapid "world-soul" of Hegel, or any other philosophical concoction, that confronts us. It isn't humanity become God, either. It is God made a Man, one human being. That this Man is God and has a Heart, worse wounded than ours, cuts off all flights into impersonal subterfuges.

In such an interview, sin can no longer be imagined as merely a creative limitation automatically outgrown in the course of some dialectical "becoming." It's no growing-pain, mere struggle, or hang-up, or chronic maladjustment, or the work of rotten parents and bad environment. In the light of that blazing, broken Heart, sin can be seen for what it is: a personal hurt maliciously, selfishly directed against Someone who loves us, and whom in all decency we should love in return.

For those who dare to venture into such intimacy, there can be only one reaction: a consuming need to make it up to Him, to love Him, to console Him for what we have done to Him. *That* is devotion to the Sacred Heart. When this point is reached, the "practices" suggest themselves. And what is such as He requested of St. Margaret Mary? And why only Thursday? On First Fridays, where sacramental Holy Communion isn't possible, spiritual Communion is always available, then and every day. The Church even attaches a three years' Indulgence to it!

"For thus says the Lord God: Behold I myself will seek my sheep, and will visit them!" *(Ezech. 34:11)*.

As St. John of the Cross said, in the evening of this life—and perhaps this world—we shall be judged on love. Opportunities for pious works don't always exist, not does God always desire them of us, but where He does desire them, they are effects of love, not its cause. "You are my friends if you do the things I command you" *(John 15:14)*. To love is to want to please the beloved by doing everything He wants us to do—and by not doing what He doesn't want us to do.

Love for the Sacred Heart drives us headlong to prayer and the Gospels in order to find out what He wants, what the "thought of His Heart" really is in any given circumstance. Love demands knowledge of its object, and in return, knowledge increases love. To be drawn into such an exchange with the Sacred Heart is to identify with the Son of God in His exchanges with His Father and the Holy Ghost in the Most Blessed Trinity. This, not "world brotherhood," is the more abundant life He promised to give to "as many as received Him" *(John 1:12)*.

From divine charity, which is love for God, in God, through God and from God, love for our fellow man follows by organic necessity. It is because our Lord loved the Father that He "by the will of the Father, with the cooperation of the Holy Ghost, has by His death given life to the world," as Holy Mass has declared through the centuries. As true man He was no more able to love other men without first loving God than we are. This must be so, because it was God who first loved us and created us, and not we Him. Without Him we can do nothing, but especially not love our fellow creatures. You would think anybody would know that.

Because so few do, Ezechiel was sent to tell us what is bound to happen: Avenging angels will be commanded:

> Go through the midst of the city, through the midst of Jerusalem: and mark Thau upon the foreheads of the men that sigh and mourn for all the abominations that are committed in the midst thereof. ... Utterly destroy old and young, maidens, children and women: but upon whomever you shall see Thau, kill him not, and begin ye at my sanctuary. So they began at the ancient men who were before the house. And he said to them: Defile the house, and fill the courts with the slain.

This is a terrifying allegory, understood in spiritual terms by those who can read the signs of the times. There need be no surprise at the wholesale defections in the Church's hierarchy. God promised here that He would "begin at the sanctuary" with the "ancient men," permitting the "house" itself to be defiled in punishment for sins against Him. Nor will the man in the pew be overlooked, for Ezechiel also tells us that the angels from the house "went forth and slew them that were in the city." No one escapes the purification God ordains, although like the prophet we may well fall on our faces crying, "Alas, alas, alas, O Lord God, wilt thou then destroy all the remnant of Israel, by pouring out thy fury upon Jerusalem?" *(Ezech.9:4,6-8)*.

Let those who "sigh and mourn for all the abominations" of the New Idolatry take heart. "For you yourselves know perfectly," says St. Paul, "that the day of the Lord shall so come as a thief in the night." All the phony peace, joy, renewal, and rights of man being currently celebrated may be a good sign, for,

> ...when they shall say, peace and security, then shall sudden destruction come upon them as the pains upon her that is with child, and they shall not escape. But you, brethren, are not in darkness, that day should overtake you as a thief ... For God has not appointed us unto wrath, but unto the purchasing of salvation by our Lord Jesus Christ, who died for us; that whether we watch or sleep, we may live together with him *(1 Thess. 5:2-10 passim.)*.

But where shall we go while all this is going on, if the sanctuary itself is desecrated?

That's easy. Ezechiel tells us God promised His faithful remnant: "*I will be to them a little sanctuary* in the countries whither they are come!" *(Ezech. 11:16)*.

This little sanctuary, foretold to the prophet and found wherever the remnant happens to be, can be nothing other than the Sacred Heart of Jesus. The true Church could never be found anywhere else. If this be so, as St. Paul said:

> Who then shall separate us from the love of Christ? Shall tribulation? or distress? or famine? or nakedness? or danger? or persecution? or the sword? ... Nor height nor depth, nor any other creature, shall be able to separate us from the love of God, which is in Christ Jesus our Lord!" *(Rom. 8:35,39)*.

The Sacred Heart establishes once and for all the primacy of the inner life. It is the absolute emblem of interiority, its strength and intensity, a citadel of prayer immediately recognized as such by those who strive to worship the Father in spirit and in truth. Because it draws us inevitably deeper into the spirit of the law away from its mere letter, the Heart of God offers unshakable shelter where all other structures collapse. Why not establish ourselves there to begin with?

It is impossible to be Christians after our Lord's own heart without imitating the hidden life He lived on earth for our example. Until the age of thirty He chose to perform no outward act that would call special attention to himself, remaining, St. John Eudes says, "withdrawn into the Father, in Whom His mind, heart, thoughts, desires and affections were uninterruptedly enclosed." He chose this in accordance with His hidden life from all eternity in the bosom of the Father, and to teach us that solitude and retirement are pleasing to God. Even during His public life He never departed from His true home in the Godhead, and if we are to become like Him we must dwell in like manner in His Sacred Heart, whatever our duties of state.

There we can always rejoice. After all, St. John Eudes reminds us, "Jesus is always Jesus, always God, always great and worthy of love, always in the same unchanging state of glory, joy and contentment, and there is nothing capable of lessening His joy and bliss. 'Know ye that the Lord he is God.' Say to Him: O Jesus, it is enough for me merely to know that you are ever Jesus! O Jesus, be Jesus forever, and I will be happy, no matter what happens to me!"

Here is personal integration on the highest possible level.

Countless Acts of Consecration have been made to the Sacred Heart of Jesus in modern times, the one by Bl. Claude de la Colombière among the first. Convinced of the veracity and urgency of St. Margaret Mary's revelations, he set down the following on June 21, 1675. Devoid of all useless preoccupation with social issues that didn't concern him, it is a model personal response from the truly generous soul of a saint our Lord Himself called His "faithful servant and perfect friend."

CONSECRATION TO THE HEART OF JESUS
By Blessed Claude de la Colombière, S.J.

To make reparation for so many outrages and such cruel ingratitude, O most adorable and lovable Heart of my lovable Jesus, and to avoid falling, as far as it is in my power to do so, into a like misfortune, I offer You my heart with all the movements of which it is capable. I give myself entirely to You, and from this hour I protest most sincerely, I think, that I desire to forget myself and all that can have any connection with me. I wish to remove the obstacle which could prevent my entering into this divine Heart which You have had the goodness to enter, there to live and die with Your faithful servants, entirely penetrated and inflamed with Your love.

I offer to this Heart all the merit, all the satisfaction of all the Masses, of all the prayers, of all the mortifications, of all the religious practices, of all the acts of zeal, of humility, of obedience and of all the other virtues which I shall practice up to the last moment of my life. Not only all this will be to honor the Heart of Jesus and its wonderful dispositions, but again I pray Him to accept the complete gift which I make to Him to dispose of as He pleases, and in favor of whomsoever He pleases. As I have already yielded to the holy souls in Purgatory all that there is in my actions that is capable of satisfying divine justice, I desire that this will be distributed to them according to the good pleasure of the Heart of Jesus.

This will not prevent me from discharging the obligations I have of saying Masses and of praying for certain intentions which obedience prescribes; or from giving through charity

Masses to poor people or to my brethren or friends who may ask them of me. But as I shall then be making use of a good that does not belong to me, I intend, as it is only just, that obedience, charity and other virtues which I shall practice on these occasions, belong to the Heart of Jesus, in which I shall find the strength to practice these virtues, which consequently will belong to Him without reserve.

Sacred Heart of Jesus, teach me perfect forgetfulness of self, since that is the only way by which one can find entrance into You. As all that I shall do in the future shall be yours, grant that I do nothing that will be unworthy of You. Teach me what I ought to do to come to the purity of Your love, the desire of which You have breathed into me. I feel in myself a tremendous inclination to please You, and a great impotence of succeeding without a great light and a special help which I can expect only from You.

Lord, do Your will in me. I well know that I oppose it. But I dearly wish, I think, not to oppose it. It is yours to do all, divine Heart of Jesus Christ. You alone will have all the glory of my sanctification if I become holy. That seems to me clearer than the day. But for You it will be a great glory, and it is for that reason alone that I would desire to be perfect. *Amen, Amen.*

Some ten years after Fr. de la Colombière composed this, the "Seraph of Paray" herself passed on the following short but fiery formula to a sister in religion. It can be ours:

SHORT ACT OF CONSECRATION
By St. Margaret Mary Alacoque

I, _____, give and consecrate to the Sacred Heart of our Lord Jesus Christ my person and my life, my actions, trials and sufferings, so that I may no longer wish to make use of any part of my being except to honor, love and glorify Him. This is my irrevocable will, to belong entirely to Him and to do everything for His love, and I renounce with all my heart anything that can be displeasing to Him. I take You, then, O Sacred Heart, as the sole object of my love, the protector of my life, the pledge of my salvation, the remedy for my infirmities, the reparation for all the sins of my life and my sure refuge at the hour of death.

Be, then, O Heart of Goodness, my justification with God the Father, and turn aside the blows of His just wrath. O Heart of Love, I place all my confidence in You. I fear everything from my malice but hope everything from Your goodness. Consume in me everything that can displease or resist You. May Your pure love impress You so deeply in my heart that I can never forget You, or ever be separated from You. I conjure You by Your boundless goodness to write my name in Your Sacred Heart, for I wish to live and die as Your slave. *Amen.*

VIII. HEART OF HEARTHS

No one insisted more than St. Margaret Mary that devotion to the Sacred Heart must not be limited to individual piety, profound as this might be. Nor was our Lord's "burning thirst to be honored by men" to be restricted to worship in churches.

She wrote:

> He has much greater plans, which can be put into effect only by His almighty power, which can accomplish whatever it wills. It seems to me He wishes to enter with pomp and magnificence into the homes of princes and kings, to be honored there to the extent He has been outraged.

In other words, He wished to establish His loving rule over human society by being acknowledged as true Head of every family, from the highest on down. The divine request was supposedly transmitted at the time to King Louis XIV, but if so, nothing came of it. The Sun King continued on the disastrous course of secular glorification which eventually produced the French Revolution, and now Marxist tyranny. One by one the nations of the world have said, "We will not have this Man to reign over us!" *(Luke 19:14)*.

The world has now reached the point that the very laws of nature are being ignored, if not outright repealed. Based on the false principle that power comes from below, a giant mechanism of organized disorder has been erected where the bond-woman Hagar habitually and by law dictates to her mistress Sarah. No one knows his proper place, because it can't be found.

Money manipulators who should be the hired servants of politics and economics are in fact formulating government policies—and that on an international level. Schools are laying down the law to parents, the family itself now the puppet of the state designed by God to serve it. Publishers determine what authors shall write. Manufacturers condition the consumer to the goods they produce. Agriculture, the sovereign human art, is indentured to industrial production, made to follow factory methods and objectives. The sovereignty of nations themselves is being absorbed into an artificial super-State organized on purely rational lines. Needless to say, the members of Holy Mother Church, already weakened and divided by the "reforms" of the so-called Reformation, are falling prostrate before the scourges of the New Order, apparently powerless to rise and protest.

With vices made law, murder of the unborn, the sick and the aged are now a matter of policy. Militant atheism, knowing no king but Caesar, is assuming all the prerogatives of a state religion. Small wonder that in such an anti-theocracy the people who long ago killed or emasculated their kings are now turning upon their own elected representatives to hasten the final triumph of perfect "freedom."

How to establish the rule of the Sacred Heart in such contrived chaos? As St. Margaret Mary saw long before the French Revolution, only God's omnipotence can accomplish a task of this proportion. Exactly how He will do it is His secret, but do it He will. "What are you afraid of?" He asked her. "I shall reign in spite of Satan and all opposition."

If His past methods are any precedent, however, He will use as His instruments the same "little ones" in all ranks of society He has always used to confound the wise of this world. St. Margaret Mary in fact predicted this: "He gave me to understand," she wrote to her Superior Mother de Saumaise, "that He does not need human power for that, because the devotion and reign of the Sacred Heart will be consolidated only by subjects poor and contemptible, amid contradictions, so that none of it can be attributed to human potential."

As always, He will scatter the proud in the conceit of their heart, putting down the mighty from their seat and exalting the humble, filling the hungry with good things and sending the rich away empty *(Luke 1:51-53)*. Until then they need only remain in His Sacred Heart, attentive to its every beat, careful to follow its manifest directives. He will tell them what to do, even though for the time being the fulfillment of His magnificent promises remains blocked by the malicious authority of the great ones of this world.

Things being as they are, about the only unit of temporal government left to us that can be brought under the sway of Christ is the private home. Furthermore, for many of us it may be the only place of worship we have left outside the privacy of our own souls. For which God be thanked, for that is exactly what a home is designed by God to be: a domestic economy over which God presides, where He is praised by its members. If home is where the heart is, then the Christian home must be where the Sacred Heart is.

Rediscovering this truth may be one of the greatest blessings He means to draw from the wanton destruction of parishes and parliaments. It's a beginning. At home Christians can still share the "one heart" which God promised Jeremiah He would give to His people, "and one way, that they may fear me all days: and that it may be well with them, and with their children after them" *(32:39)*.

The Acts of the Apostles relate how "the multitude of believers had but one heart and one soul: neither did anyone say that aught of the things which he possessed was his own: but all things were common unto them" *(4:32)*. This "one heart" of saints who lovingly share all they possess is today in open confrontation with the "one world" of androids intent on robbing one another of even the most elementary right to private ownership. There can be no co-existence between the two.

We cannot repeat too often that devotion to the Sacred Heart, promulgated from the very first as a devotion for the latter times, is now only beginning. What has been achieved so far is the merest preparation or predisposition for a fullness yet to be even suspected. It would be ridiculous to think our Lord hasn't foreseen and provided for all the deprivations we are facing—the desecration of Churches, suppression of sacred images and sacramentals, the defections of the priesthood, or worst of all, the disappearance of the Holy Sacrifice itself along with the Sacraments.

We have noted already that devotion to the Sacred Heart has established once and for all the primacy of the interior life. What it does for the individual in his own soul it is equally prepared to do for society, in the home. We start where we can. Is there any reason why what our Lord requested of worldly monarchs can't be accorded Him by lesser heads of families? Let those who preach "power to the people" beware of that power when it is brandished in the service of God!

What is to prevent exposing and honoring the picture of the Sacred Heart in our homes—if only because "wherever this holy picture should be exposed to be honored, He would lavish His graces and blessings"? Better still, why not satisfy at home our Lord's longing to be adored in the Blessed Sacrament? That Benediction has all but disappeared from the liturgy, or that the Church doors are locked, or that the Sacrament itself may no longer be reserved, can be seen to be no excuse at all when we look deeply into the matter.

One of the first to see this was the late Fr. Mateo Crawley-Boevey, of the Congregation of the Sacred Hearts of Jesus and Mary, who initiated the movement for Enthronement of the Sacred Heart in the home. With truly prophetic insight he began preaching Eucharistic Adoration as a practice most proper to the home. Already in the late 1920's he was signing up families for one hour a month of night adoration, at a time when the Real Presence was taken for granted in every Catholic church and expected to continue there until the end of the world.

Fr. Mateo may not have been so sure. He wrote:

> We are in fact on the brink of an abyss of social corruption; the home already undermined in its very foundations by this upheaval of immorality; a good part of the portion of society which

by right is considered the best, the most Christian, seriously affected by the contagion of unbridled sensuality ... What is sadder still, the enemy has now penetrated into our own ranks; the wolf is encountered with unheard of cruelty in a full sheepfold. More, he is tolerated there, even encouraged by the cowardice of friends. Thus Satan and the world have without pity struck and scourged their God and their Lord. His very bones might be counted through His wounds, for 'there is no soundness in Him.'

Urging reparation to the Sacred Heart, his practical suggestions for domestic adoration are very instructive:

> In large families the adoration may be arranged in such a way that each member of the family watches in turn before a picture of the Sacred Heart. If the Sacred Heart has been enthroned in the home, then the adoration should take place before the enthroned picture of the Sacred Heart, around which lighted candles and flowers have been placed, if this is possible and practical ... The adoration should be made as far as possible on one's knees, in a spirit of salutary penance ... It should be throughout a Eucharistic Adoration, in spirit and in truth. Picture to yourself the walls of His sacramental prison, and contemplate our King and Prisoner of Love in the complete solitude and abandonment of the tabernacle; in this Gethsemane He will be consoled by the chalice of sweetness offered to Him by the adoring soul.

How much better this than wasting prayer time in some Church where there may be good reason to wonder whether the host in the tabernacle is actually Consecrated? And we can still have with us holy water, blessed candles, statues, medals and other sacramentals. There are the Rosary, the Litanies, and other approved prayers of the Church, not to mention our knees. Outstanding among such helps would be a copy of the Holy Face from the Shroud of Turin, so intimately associated with devotion to the Sacred Heart in its very origin on Calvary. The radiance of this divine Countenance is perhaps the closest thing we have here on earth to that of the Real Presence, its effects truly miraculous on those who contemplate it with love and gratitude. Being, we might say, the official portrait our Lord has left us of himself, it delivers the most intimate thoughts of the Sacred Heart to its beholder.

It makes His Passion ours:

> The same love which made Me suffer such extreme pains and affliction for the salvation of men, makes Me also suffer now in your heart, immortal and impassible as I am, by the intimate compassion with which it is penetrated for the salvation of my elect, in consideration of my afflictions and bitternesses. Therefore in return for the compassion which you have had for my sufferings, I give you the whole fruit of my Passion and death, to insure your eternal beatitude.

Spoken to St. Gertrude, these words make plain what meditation on the Sacred Heart is meant to lead to. Fr. Mateo suggested prayers for the following intentions during hours of home adoration:

> Our Holy Father the Pope, peace, the clergy, the members of your family who may have gone astray, those in their agony this night, the Social Reign of the Sacred Heart, particularly through the Enthronement of the Sacred Heart in the home. Oh, be true angels of Gethsemane in this nocturnal adoration, you who have an advantage over the angel from heaven, since you are able to suffer and to weep in union with the agonizing Heart of Jesus!

Most significantly, Fr. Mateo urged adorers to begin their hour by uniting themselves in spirit with the priests who at that moment might be offering the Holy Sacrifice anywhere in the world. He wished them if possible to recite the Canon of the Mass in view of a spiritual Communion, all the while adoring, praising, petitioning and atoning "through Him, with Him and in Him." If Mass can't be attended in fact, it can be attended in desire.

Aware of the importance of Fr. Mateo's latter day apostolate, Popes Benedict XV, Pius XI and Pius XII each accorded the Apostolic Benediction to those engaging in it. In his enthusiasm Pope Pius XI dubbed it "the actualization of my Encyclical"— *Miserentissimus Redemptor*, on the Sacred Heart. With such encouragement from the highest Authority, why not adore at home kneeling in spirit before our Lord's true sacramental presence in all Churches or places where It may still be found?

Isn't it this Real Presence that the image of the Sacred Heart is precisely meant to evoke in our homes? Wouldn't our Lord intend to follow His Heart's image personally into any place where it was lovingly exposed? If not, how could devotion to the Sacred Heart make any real sense? That He would accompany it spiritually seems clear, but who knows but that some day He may intend to repose there physically, sacramentally, as well?

True devotion to the Sacred Heart is no outmoded spiritual practice, but one barely begun, hardly tried. Without prying into divine secrets, we may piously hope that in the great period of peace promised by our Lady of Fatima, when our dismembered society will be reestablished under the rule of Christ the King, the Blessed Sacrament may be reserved in Christian homes as a matter of course without likelihood of profanation, as It was in the early days of the Church's fervor. Until then the image alone of the Sacred Heart must continue to plead from our firesides. It is Christ's own prayer to God the Father, one He cannot ignore.

CONSECRATION OF THE FAMILY TO THE SACRED HEART OF JESUS

Sacred Heart of Jesus, You revealed to St. Margaret Mary Your desire to reign over Christian families. To fulfill this desire we today proclaim Your complete dominion over our family. From now on we wish to live Your life, to cultivate in our home those virtues which bring with them Your peace, and to avoid that worldliness which we have condemned. You will rule over our minds by simple faith and over our hearts by a love kept aflame by frequent Holy Communion.

Divine Heart of Jesus, be pleased to preside over our family, to bless all we do, to dispel our troubles, sanctify our joys, lighten our sufferings. If one of us should ever offend You by sin, remind him, merciful Jesus, of your goodness and mercy to the penitent sinner. And when the hour for separation strikes, when death brings its grief into our midst, those of us who go and those who must stay will be submissive to what you have decreed. Then it will be our consolation to remember that the day will come when our entire family, reunited in Heaven, will be able to sing forever of Your glory and Your mercy.

May the Immaculate Heart of Mary and the glorious patriarch St. Joseph present to You this consecration of ours and keep us ever mindful of it all the days of our life. All Glory to the Sacred Heart of Jesus, our King and our Father!

IX. ONE IN HEART

But there's more.

It's not good for the Sacred Heart of the new Adam to be alone. Like Adam's, it too must be joined by the new Eve's.

St. John Eudes used to say that Jesus and Mary are so closely bound together that whoever beholds the Son beholds the Mother, and that whoever loves the one cannot help loving the other. We must not separate what God has so perfectly joined together. There is no pleasing God without honoring the Blessed Virgin in union with His Son, taking delight in what He takes delight in. So necessary is she to our salvation, well have saints smelled reprobation in souls lacking devotion to her!

Not only does God disapprove of honoring His Son without her, but St. John Eudes insisted the Blessed Virgin herself disapproved of it. So closely are they united, he considered it a serious mistake even to depict one without the other. To admit the possibility of conforming oneself to one without the other is heresy, not to mention bad psychology. To become like Christ we must love what he loves, and whom did he love more than His Immaculate Mother?

As *forma Dei*, the mold from which God chose to produce himself in flesh here below, she is indispensable to our sanctification. As St. Louis de Montfort, that great apostle of Mary put it, God "did not disdain to shut himself up in the womb of the Blessed Virgin, as a captive and as a loving slave, and later to be subject to her for thirty years." We must love her therefore as He does, with His very own Heart which has loved her from the beginning, and indeed created the whole material universe in view of her Queenship over us. How could we dare enthrone the Sacred Heart on the Feast of Christ the King without acknowledging her rule as well?

That such is God's will is evident. It's no coincidence that St. Margaret Mary and St. John Eudes were contemporaries, or that years before our Lord appeared to the Visitandine, St. John was preaching public devotion to the Sacred Hearts. In 1674, at the very time of the apparitions at Paray-le-Monial, the Confraternity of the Sacred Heart of Jesus and the Most Pure Heart of Mary established by him was approved by Pope Clement X and enriched with indulgences.

Venerable Mary of Agreda, who wrote our Lady's biography under her dictation, has some interesting information to relay in *The Mystical City of God.* Our Lady told her that at the beginning of our Lord's public ministry she "gave thanks to the eternal Father for the first disciples, and in spirit recognized and accepted them as her spiritual sons, being also our Lord's and offered them to the divine majesty with new songs of praise and rejoicing of spirit. "

We are told our Lord began His instructions to the first five Apostles by acquainting them with His miraculous Incarnation in His Mother's womb, for it was necessary,

> ...that they know her and venerate her as true Mother and Virgin ... On such catechism and heavenly doctrine were the Savior's first sons fed. Before entering the presence of the great Queen they were well aware of her divine preeminence, knowing she was a virgin before, during and after childbirth; and Christ our Lord filled them with deep reverence and love, so that from that very moment they aspired to see and become acquainted with so divine a creature ... These first five disciples begged our lord to grant them the consolation of meeting and paying their respects to His Mother, and acceding to their wishes, He travelled straight to Nazareth on entering Galilee ...

La Venerable continues:

It was a marvel of divine omnipotence, a wonder among wonders how our most prudent Lady Mary dealt with the sacred college of the holy Apostles and disciples of our Lord Christ, her most holy Son. Such rare wisdom cannot be put into words, but even if I tried to divulge all I was given to understand about it, it would be necessary to write a huge volume on this subject alone ... Into the hearts of all the disciples He admitted to His divine school was poured a special devotion and reverence for His most holy Mother, as was proper, inasmuch as they were to see and treat with her so familiarly in His company.

Nevertheless, although the implantation of divine light was common to all, it wasn't the same in each; because His Majesty distributed these gifts according to the Lord's dispensation, the dispositions of the recipients, and the ministries and functions He destined them for. And later, given the society and wonderfully delightful conversation of the great Queen, they kept increasing in reverent love and esteem for her, because she spoke with them all, loving, consoling, listening, instructing and helping them in all their difficulties, so that they never left her presence and conversation without being filled with interior joy, gladness and consolation beyond anything they could desire.

Our Lady further confided to Agreda that among the divine secrets her Son revealed to the beloved Apostle John the night of the Last Supper was that he enjoyed the Savior's special favor in return for the love he had shown His Mother, whereas on the other hand Judas was lost for having scorned the intercession she offered him. It is impossible to please God without accepting, at least implicitly, the tutelage of our Lady. Even in her lifetime on earth, says Agreda, "the office of Mother and Teacher of the holy Church, which the Lord had conferred upon most holy Mary, was necessarily accompanied by a knowledge and light proportionate to those high offices."

Viewed thus, our Lady might be considered, like the Church, as a near incarnation of the Holy Ghost:

For she was to know all the members of this Mystical Body which she governed, so that she might apply her teachings and her ministrations according to each one's station, condition and necessity ... She knew all the faithful that joined the Church, was informed of the natural inclinations, of the degree of virtue and grade they possessed, the merit of their works, their beginning and end. She was ignorant of nothing pertaining to the Church, except sometimes when the Lord concealed from her some affair which afterwards was made known to her at its conclusion.

...But the Mother of fair love and knowledge did not pervert the order of distributive justice, mixing in her affections; she dispensed it by the light of the Lamb, who enlightened and governed her, dealing out her heartfelt love to each according to his merits, neither more nor less. ... The great Queen was most solicitous to show unbiased and uniform favor to all the members of the Church in public. This conduct was not only worthy of such a mistress, but most necessary in the beginnings of her government. For the principles upon which her behavior was founded were to be well established for the guidance of prelates in the future government of the Church.

It would be impossible to enumerate all the sacred authorities who from apostolic times have urged us to add devotion to the Heart of Mary to that of her Son. In due time their admonitions were summed up by our Lady herself, who in 1830 granted St. Catherine Labouré a vision of the Miraculous Medal, whereon the Hearts of Jesus and Mary were shown side by side. At Fatima in 1917 she said straight out that God desired her heart to be venerated with His, and that it was to her Immaculate Heart in particular that the peace of the world was entrusted. It would, she promised, triumph in the end. Pope Pius XII consecrated the whole world to her Heart, magnifying the consecration to the Sacred Heart pronounced by his predecessor Leo XIII.

Not that devotion to our Lady's Heart is an invention of modern times. Like devotion to the sacred Heart of Jesus, its main lines can be discerned even in the old Testament, especially in the "wisdom" books, climaxing in Canticles. There we read of God's bride who "sleeps" but whose "heart watches," and who begs Christ to "put me as a seal upon thy heart" in a mystical exchange bespeaking the Incarnation *(Cant. 5:2; 8:6)*.

St. John Eudes shows that devotion to the Immaculate Heart is actually rooted in the Gospels. Mary's heart is mentioned by

St. Luke even before our Lord's. At Jesus' birth in Bethlehem, when "all who heard marveled at the things told them by the shepherds ... Mary kept in mind all these words, pondering them in her heart" *(Luke 2:18-19)*. Twelve years later, returning from Jerusalem after finding her Son in the Temple, Mary is said to have "kept all these things carefully in her heart" *(Luke 2:51)*.

St. Luke so noted, writes St. John Eudes, because,

> ...the Holy Ghost, who dictated to the holy Evangelists everything they wrote, willed that one of them speak to us with proper reverence of the Heart of the Mother of the Savior, depicting it to us as the sacred repository and faithful custodian of the ineffable mysteries and priceless treasures contained in the wonderful life of this divine Redeemer, no doubt so that by imitating it we may render this august Heart the eternal homage which is its due.

Even more significant is St. Luke's account of the infant Lord's Presentation in the Temple, where the aged priest Simeon tells the Blessed Mother, "And thy own soul a sword shall pierce, that the thoughts of many hearts may be revealed" *(Luke 2:35)*. Already in Patristic times it was understood that this "sword" transfixed her heart, for it was from this passage that the popular representations of Mary's heart which are now so familiar to us were originally adapted and developed.

Mary's conformity to Christ, however, went far beyond that of a mere repository of His mysteries. Her role in His life didn't stop with the Incarnation at Nazareth. St. Brigid of Sweden, destined in the fourteenth century to receive private revelations on this subject, says our Lady told her:

> When He suffered, I felt as though my heart endured the sufferings also ... When my Son was scourged and torn with whips, my heart was scourged and whipped with Him ... *His Heart was my heart* ... so that my beloved Son and I redeemed the world as with one Heart *(Revelations, Bk.1, Ch.35)*.

Needless to say it was on Calvary, where the Sacred Heart of Jesus burst open, that Simeon's prophecy was consummated. St.

John tells us that "when they saw that he was already dead ... one of the soldiers with a spear opened his side" *(St. John 19:33-34)*. Well may we suspect along with the Fathers of the Church that this spear wielded by St. Longinus was the sword Simeon predicted would one day pierce Mary's soul, to her very heart. Our Lord was already dead. The physical pain of the blow could no longer reach Him, but it did reach her, still standing at the foot of the Cross. She it was who suffered this gratuitous wound, her heart bursting open mystically with her Son's for the sins of men in an excess of love. The Passion of Christ did not end on the Cross, but in the Immaculate Heart of His Mother, who with Him is co-Redemptrix of the world.

There is profound mystery here. As we have seen, our Lord told St. Catherine of Siena that He was struck after death "for several reasons." There can be no doubt that the perfecting of His Mother's com-Passion was one of them. Mary's suffering was not merely vicarious, a deeply sympathetic hurt such as is naturally experienced at the sight of damage inflicted on someone very close to us. As our Lady explained to St. Brigid, "His Heart was my heart." No man and woman were ever "one flesh" to the extent that she and her Son were.

Ven. Mary of Agreda tells us that her conformity to the divine will was such that the Incarnation itself had been entirely an affair of the heart. At the moment of her *fiat*,

> ...her most pure heart, as it were by natural consequence, was contracted and compressed with such force, that it distilled three drops of her most pure blood, and these finding their way to the natural place for the act of conception, were formed by the power of the divine and holy Spirit into the body of Christ our Lord. Thus the matter from which the most holy Humanity of the Word for our Redemption is composed, was furnished and administered by the most pure heart of Mary and through the sheer force of her true love.

No human father having taken part in our Lord's conception, His flesh was derived entirely from hers, His human Heart produced exclusively from her own by divine power. We can even say that in its natural components the Most Precious Blood

He shed for us was to some extent hers. This is one reason we can speak with theological accuracy of the necessity of making reparation to the Heart of Mary as well as to the Heart of Jesus. She herself has asked that we offer the First Saturday of every month for this intention. This is further due her not only as Mediatrix of all graces pouring from the Savior's breast, but most of all as co-redemptrix by right of her suffering, joined voluntarily, mystically to His.

Our Lady once had to reassure Venerable Mary of Agreda concerning a startling intuition she had received of the presence of the Mother of God in the Tabernacle. Telling her to be assiduous in imitating her devotion to the Blessed Sacrament, our Lady added:

> Observe also that which you have added yourself in order to do reverence to the sacramental Flesh and Blood as coming from my womb and as having been nourished and grown from my milk. Ever keep up this devotion, for the truth you have perceived, that this consecrated Body contains part of my own blood and substance, is in fact real.

True devotion to the Immaculate Heart of Mary therefore is devotion to the Sacred Heart of Jesus. What does Mary want? Consecration to the Sacred Heart. What does our Lord want? Consecration to the Immaculate Heart of His Mother. Where devotion is genuine, one leads inevitably to the other; and where it does not, the devotion is spurious, no matter how authentic it may look.

Said Mother Mary Potter, foundress of the latter day Congregation of the Little Company of Mary:

> On Calvary, Mary came forward more prominently than at any other time of her life. So is she coming forward more prominently at this time, when the Church is, as it were, on Calvary. May many of her children receive the holy vocation to imitate their Mother and stand with her on Calvary, pleading in union with her by the blood her heart had furnished, the Precious Blood of Jesus shed with so great love to give life to the souls of men!

In this Heart may we all be one.

BIBLIOGRAPHY

Bainvel, J., S.J., *Devotion to the Sacred Heart*, Burns Oates and Washbourne, 1924.

Barbet, Pierre, *A Doctor Looks at Calvary*, Image Books, Garden City, N.Y., 1963.

Beauchesne, Gabriel, *Sainte Marguerite-Marie, Sa Vie Intime*, Rue de Rennes 117, Paris, 1931.

Crawley-Boevey, Mateo, SSCC, *Holy Hour for Night Adoration in the Home*, National Center of the Enthronement, Washington, D.C., 1944.

Eudes, St. John, *Le Coeur Admirable de la Très Sacrée Mère de Dieu*, Paris, 1908.

Herambourg, Peter, CJM, *St. John Eudes*, (Hauser translation), Newman Press, 1960.

Herbst, Clarence A., *The Letters of Saint Margaret Mary Alacoque*, Henry Regnery Co., Chicago, 1954.

Life and Revelations of St. Gertrude, Newman Press, Westminster, Md., 1952.

Maria de Jesus de Agreda, Ven. Sor, *Mystica Ciudad de Dios*, Herederos de Juan Gili, 5 vols, Barcelona, 1911.

Maria de Jesus de Agreda, Ven. Sor, *The City of God* (Fiscar Marison translation), Ave Maria Institute, Washington, N.J., 1971.

Merton, Thomas, OCSO, *What Are These Wounds?*, Bruce Publishing Co., 1950.

Pius XII, *Haurietis aquas*, Encyclical, 1956.

Potter, Mother Mary, *Mary's Conferences, Congregation of the Little Company of Mary*, Chicago, 1965.

Stierli, J., *Heart of the Savior*, Herder and Herder, 1957.

Thorold, Algar, *The Dialogue of St. Catherine of Siena*, Newman Press, Westminster, Md.,1950.

Young, William J. S.J., *Faithful Servant, Spiritual Retreats and Letters of Blessed Claude de la Colombière*, Herder, 1960.

Quotations from Holy Scripture are taken from the Rheims-Douai translation of the Vulgate.

THE HOLY ROSARY: ULTIMATE LITURGY

I.

There is no mention whatever of the Rosary in the documents of the Second Vatican Council. Not even in the Dogmatic Constitution *Lumen Gentium*, whose final chapter deals exclusively with our Lady's role in the Church. A vague reference in Article 67 to "practices and exercises of devotion towards her" might be assumed to include it, but according to Bishop Rendeiro of Coïmbra, the Bishops who wished to add to the text "the Rosary with meditation on the Mysteries of the life of Christ and the Blessed Virgin" were voted down. Apparently the Council deemed it best to follow the recommendations of the Theological Commission and make no mention of particular devotions, for fear of encouraging manifestations of piety beyond what they termed "the limits of sound and orthodox doctrine."[1]

Fr. Avery Dulles, who wrote an interesting introduction to this decree for one of its English translations, says that "a separate document on the Blessed Virgin was contemplated, and was presented in draft form by the Theological Commission at the first session in 1962. But the Fathers saw a danger in treating Mariology too much in isolation ..." The decree reads, "This Synod earnestly exhorts theologians and preachers of the divine word that in treating of the unique dignity of the Mother of God, they carefully and equally avoid the falsity of exaggeration on the one hand and the excess of narrow-mindedness on the other."

Not for them the beloved adage of the saints, "*De Maria numquam satis!*" They were solicitous to "painstakingly guard against any word or deed which could lead separated brethren or

---

[1] Guy Le Rumeur, *Marie et la Grande Hérésie*, 79290 Argenton-l'Église, 1974, pp. 20-1.

anyone else into error regarding the true doctrine of the Church."
They would only concede that the Church "has endorsed many
forms of piety toward the Mother of God," forms which "have
varied according to the circumstances of time and place and have
reflected the diversity of native characteristics and temperament
among the faithful."

There are certainly many devotions of this kind throughout
the Catholic world, but it would be impossible to locate the
Rosary among them, for this unique prayer has never been tied to
any time, place or people, nor did it arise from any particular
human culture. Like all true liturgy, it had no earthly origin.
Saints have believed that our Lord himself proposed it to the
Apostles.

In point of fact the Rosary began at the foot of the Cross
along with Sacred Heart devotion. When Our Lady appeared to
St. Dominic with instructions to propagate the Rosary, she did so
for the same reason that our Lord would one day appear to St.
Margaret Mary. In neither case was anything new proposed to
the faithful, who were merely being recalled to practices known
in the Church from the beginning, but which they were in
imminent danger of forgetting.

One of the strongest indications of the Rosary's supernatural
character is its ability to withstand human manipulation. Amid
the diabolic disorientation unleashed by the "Spirit of Vatican
II," it was only natural to expect that those who believe worship
should conform to the times rather than the wishes of the Holy
Ghost would lay hands on the Rosary as they had on the liturgy.
The repetitive character of the prayer was deemed particularly
unsuited to the mature modern mentality. By God's grace and
our Lady's protection, however, so far every attempt to create a
New Rosary has come to nought.

Like the traditional Mass, the traditional Rosary has been
suppressed,   denigrated   and   ignored,   but   never   entirely

eliminated. Even adaptations like the "Scriptural Rosary" still being promoted have never become really popular. As it became increasingly evident to the Rosary's devotees that to tamper with it was to tamper with God's work, the only strategy left to the innovators was to disregard it as much as possible.

A movement to omit the Angelic Salutation from the Hail Mary and say the second part only was indignantly repudiated by the late Bishop Venancio of Fatima and finally scotched in 1973 by an international Blue Army seminar meeting in India. In its closing session Archbishop Dominic Athaide of Agra was unanimously supported in a motion to petition the Pope to retain the Hail Mary in its entirety. The following year, however, the Concilium of the Legion of Mary was prevailed upon to instruct its chapters to experiment in updating the Rosary. Strongly suggested was the reduction of each five decades of the Rosary to four.

This involved combining some of the traditional mysteries into one and adding two extra sets of Mysteries: the "Hopeful," in which figured among other novelties the first prophecy of Jeremias on the Redemption and the birth and espousals of Our Lady; and some "Mysteries of Oblation" highlighting the Flight into Egypt and the three days' loss of Jesus. A complete Rosary, which traditionally contains 3 sets of Mysteries, would therefore have 5 sets, requiring 200 Hail Marys instead of the usual 150, with each set requiring only 40 Hail Marys instead of 50. What a master ploy on the part of the enemy had it succeeded! Overnight every Rosary in existence would have been obsolete!

All the while conceding that the Rosary's major components, the Angelic Salutation and the Our Father, figure prominently in the Gospels, its adversaries are wont to deny its authenticity by pointing out that the Rosary itself is nowhere mentioned in Scripture. These cavilers are perhaps best refuted by St. Basil's famous sermon on "Sacred Tradition as Divine Guide" :

> Of the beliefs and public doctrines entrusted to the care of the Church, there are some which are based on Scriptural teaching, others which we have received handed down in mystery by the tradition of the Apostles; and in relation to the true religion they

both have the same force. Nor is there anyone will contradict them; no one certainly who has the least acquaintance with the established laws of the Church. For were we to attempt to reject the unwritten practices of the Church as being without great importance, we would unknowingly inflict mortal wounds on the Gospel. ...

For example ... who is it that has taught us in writing to sign with the sign of the Cross those who place their trust in Jesus Christ our Lord? ... The words of the invocation at the Consecration of the Eucharistic Bread and the Chalice of Blessing, which of the saints has left them to us in writing? For we are not content with the words both the Gospel and the Apostles have recorded, but have added some others, both before these and after them, as having great significance to the mystery, and which we have received from unwritten tradition.

Zealous demythologizers laboring to dismiss the revelation of the Rosary to St. Dominic as pious legend rest their case largely on the absence of any mention of his actually saying the Rosary in contemporary documents. But then, neither do we possess a single one of his sermons, although he founded the Order of Preachers! Leo XIII, the "Pope of the Rosary," who wrote no less than eleven encyclicals and an apostolic letter on the subject, unequivocally upheld the authenticity of the tradition. In 1891 he declared in *Octobri mense* that it was by the express "command and counsel" of the heavenly Queen "*that the devotion was begun and spread abroad by the Holy Patriarch Dominic* as a most powerful weapon against the enemies of the Faith in an epoch not unlike our own, and indeed of great danger to our holy religion."

Actually Leo XIII was only reaffirming doctrine already defined by Pope St. Pius V. Incredible as it may seem, the vast majority of Catholics are unaware that this same Pope, who canonized the Mass for all time in the famous bull *Quo primum* in 1570, had first canonized the Rosary the year before in the bull *Consueverunt*. Ratifying the tradition relating to St. Dominic and officially entrusting the propagation of the Rosary to his spiritual sons, the document defines once and for all the form in which the Rosary is to be prayed:

...respiciens modum facilem, et omnibus pervium, ac modum pium orandi et precandi Deum, Rosarium seu Psalterium eiusdem B. MARIAE VIRGINIS nuncupatum, quo eadem Beatissima Virgo Salutatione Angelica centies et quinquagesies ad numerum Davidici Psalterii repetita, et Oratione Dominica ad quamlibet decimam cum certis meditaionibus totam eiusdem D.N. Jesu Christi vitam demonstrantibus interposita, etc.

As with the Mass, St. Pius did not concoct or change anything. He merely stated with the full authority of his office what the proper form of the Rosary is, giving obedient testimony to the work of the Holy Ghost, principal author of genuine liturgy. Far from suggesting possible variations or innovations, the Holy See was at pains even then to proscribe spurious forms of the Rosary, as can be seen in its condemnation of the "Seraphic" Rosary and others like that of the Blessed Trinity and of St. Anne. A new Mass was promulgated by Paul VI, but no Pope has yet presumed to promulgate a new Rosary. Its basic form remains what St. Pius V laid down in the passage just quoted: 150 Hail Marys in groups of ten with an Our Father in between, joined to meditation on certain mysteries of the life of our Lord.

After *Consueverunt,* all variations were consistently discouraged, mostly by promoting the canonically approved form and indulgencing it ever more heavily. As in the case of the Mass, however, venerable customs of long standing were scrupulously respected. For instance, whereas Latins are accustomed to announce the proper mystery at the beginning of each decade, it had become usual in Teutonic countries to repeat it with each Hail Mary after "thy womb, Jesus." This practice was retained and allowed in those areas and persists to this day. Be it noted also that indulgences (which, incidentally, are attached to the beads and not to the chain or the string) have never been granted to any unapproved variations, "scriptural" or otherwise. Special permission was required to add the Fatima petition, "O my Jesus, forgive us our sins ... " to the end of each decade.

II.

Modernist opinion to the contrary, the Rosary is no sentimental paraliturgical practice developed by Christian folk over the centuries to keep children, little old ladies and ignorant peasants occupied with a devotion suited to their limited capacities. Whoever would consider it insufficiently "Christological" to rank with the major ecclesiastical devotions need only be reminded that the Hail Mary was the first Christian prayer. Given to the world before the Lord's Prayer, it contained the latter in embryo much as our Lady bore our Lord. As official announcement of His arrival, the climax of the Hail Mary is not praise of His Mother, but praise of "the fruit of thy womb, Jesus." Before the close of the thirteenth century the Holy Ghost had inspired the Church to add the Holy Name to the Salutation, thus making the focus on Christ explicit and unmistakable.

Although men contributed to the Rosary's development, it was not put together by men. Under divine impulsion it grew from the Archangel Gabriel's greeting to Mary as a living plant from seed. No prayer is so firmly rooted in Apostolic tradition as the Rosary. The Breton Dominican Bl. Alain de la Roche, who after two centuries would revitalize St. Dominic's work, is said to have learned in prayer that the first promoter of the practice was St. Bartholomew. Perpetuated among the Desert Fathers, it was not unknown to St. Augustine, St. Benedict, St. Bernard, St. Francis, St. Lutgard, St. Christina and many early saints.

The meditations on the fifteen principal mysteries of salvation which accompany the prayers are no modern accretions, but among the Rosary's most ancient elements. They could not have sprung from the Rosary, for they engendered it. All those who had a hand in forging its mysteries—from Mary and Joseph through St. John the Baptist, Zachary, Elizabeth, on past the ox and ass at Bethlehem to the thief on the cross, Mary

Magdalene at Christ's tomb and those first Christians in the Cenacle at Pentecost—were architects of the Rosary. Piece by piece they put it together by their faith and suffering, and all are present to the soul who contemplates their extraordinary achievement.

Rooted in the injunction to "pray without ceasing" which binds all men, the Rosary provides a method for keeping the whole person—mind, mouth and hands—occupied with God. To call it perfect liturgy is no mere figure of speech, but sober fact. Designed as it was by the Queen of heaven to facilitate prayer for those unable to recite the Divine Office, its 150 Hail Marys were first said in lieu of the 150 Davidic Psalms recited by the monks. What better substitute for meditation on the old Psalms than meditation on the very Mysteries they prefigured? On occasion the joyful, sorrowful or glorious Mysteries were enjoined as substitutes for the official Psalter when for any reason this could not be said.

So well was the Rosary's liturgical character understood, that for a long time its recitation actually began with the prayer *Aperies* as does the Office. Even today it ends with the "Hail Holy Queen," which is the ancient hymn *Salve Regina* sung at the Office's close. Whereas the great Office is the *Opus Dei*, the work of God, the Rosary may be rightly called the *Opusculum Dei*, God's little work, or at least the *Opusculum Mariae*, the little work of our Lady. In his encyclical on the Rosary Pope Pius XII does not scruple to refer to it as a "rite" to be "performed."[2]

Its preparation, both natural and supernatural, was long and careful. Counters for keeping track of prayers date from earliest antiquity and are common to many false religions, as witness those "rosaries" which St. Francis Xavier was surprised to find

[2] September 15, 1951

Japanese Buddhists using and the "worry beads" currently used by Moslems. In themselves such devices have no religious significance beyond mute testimony to original sin, which has so weakened human powers of concentration as to render them necessary. It is only through the goodness of our heavenly Mother that the Rosary has become a sacramental. Perhaps she set the Hail Marys in decades so that in emergencies baptized fingers and toes could serve.

Following a practice known in Old Testament times, early monks used knotted string, beads or small pebbles to keep track of the Psalms. Judging from evidence found in contemporary pictures, statuary, poems and hymns, these first counters were not regularly divided into sets of ten, but rather arrayed in fifties or multiples of fifty. Because Our Fathers were sometimes substituted for the Psalms when necessity demanded, they became known as "Paternoster beads." Thus after St. Dominic's time, when the Angelic Salutation and meditation on the principal mysteries of the Faith were substituted, it was only natural to refer to the Rosary as "Our Lady's Paternoster," or "Our Lady's Psalter" as did St. Pius V in his bull.

It was St. Dominic's great privilege, at our Lady's behest, to raise the systematic repetition of the Angelic Salutation to the level of official prayer. Beginning by inserting it into the Office of Our Lady for clerics, he substituted it for the Office among tertiaries and the laity, and recommended praying sets of fifties to the faithful in general. Inasmuch as these early Hail Marys were probably said on Paternoster beads, the two prayers certainly became joined in various combinations early on, but the Rosary we are familiar with did not take shape until the second half of the fifteenth century.

In his biography of St. Catherine of Siena, Bl. Raymond of Capua relates that when St. Dominic organized his tertiaries into the Militia of Jesus Christ, "The holy founder imposed on them a certain number of *Paternosters* and *Avemarias*, which they prayed instead of the canonical hours when they did not attend the Divine Office." Seven *Paters* for each of the seven Hours of the day and seven *Aves* for each Hour of Our Lady's Office were their only prayers of obligation, so that when St. Dominic's friend Pope Gregory IX officially approved the order, he automatically conferred formal recognition on the Rosary. Those forty-nine *Aves* recited by the Militia were therefore the first of the millions of "rose garlands" which the Church would offer liturgically to Mary until now.[3]

Prepared from eternity for its apocalyptic mission, the Rosary from its first appearance on earth seemed always to keep pace with surges of evil. Our Lady had appeared to St. Dominic at the very dawn of that awful spiritual cataclysm so bedecked in natural grace and glamour that we still refer to it as the Renaissance. This "rebirth" unfortunately turned out to be that of the spirit of Babel, which loosed paganism and unregenerate humanism once more over the world. Painting, music, politics, philosophy and all the arts and sciences began following their own head in concerted revolt against Christ their King and Creator.

It was to divert this noxious flood at its headwaters that the faithful had been urged to fling the Angelic Salutation into the teeth of the Cathar heresy. The enthusiastic response constituted a massive declaration of Marian faith, for denial of Mary's divine Maternity and proscription of prayer to her figured prominently among Cathar errors. Under Dominican direction St. Louis of France and St. Margaret of Hungary became ardent promoters, and the devotion spread throughout Christendom like wildfire. All Europe prayed the Hail Mary by fifties, and She who defeats all heresies granted a decisive victory.

For Bl. Alan de la Roche, "to preach the Psalter [of our Lady] is nothing else but to lead the people to devotion, penance, contempt of the world and reverence for the Church." Through his instrumentality the Rosary entered the realm of communal prayer. Religious Congregations espoused it, not merely as pious

---

[3] Luis Alonso Getino, O.P. *Origin del Rosario*, Madrid 1925.

practice, but as a means of perfection. Without losing its personal character, it provided a simple, flexible base on which any variety of associations might be formed, and after he established the first Rosary Confraternity in Douai in 1470, literally hundreds came into being. Because members were granted special indulgences at the hour of death, it was during this period that the second half of the Hail Mary was added: "Holy Mary, Mother of God, pray for us sinners now and at the hour of our death." Those who may have to face the final encounter with Satan without Holy Viaticum should be mindful of the Rosary's power *in extremis*.

Recommending daily recitation to everyone, Bl. Alan unified popular devotion in such a way that in due time the Holy See could act upon it and render it even more fruitful. Popularized by the swelling Confraternities, the Rosary was no longer limited to one religious order, but gradually became the prayer of the whole Church. It was intimately connected with the discovery of America and all that followed upon it, for missionaries carried it far beyond the boundaries of Christendom.

According to the Breviary the Turks were defeated at Lepanto "on the very day on which the Confraternities of the Most Holy Rosary throughout the world were offering up their rosaries, as they had been asked to do." The Venetian Senate went further, formally declaring, *"Non virtus, non arma, non duces, sed Maria Rosarii victores fecit,"* attributing their success not to bravery, arms or leadership, but exclusively to the power of Our Lady of the Rosary. A second victory over the Turks was won through her intercession a century later at Vienna, and again in the next century at Belgrade. By then "Rosario" had become a common baptismal name.

Although for a long time conforming to the seven liturgical Hours, the Rosary had gradually become distinct from the Office proper and was pursuing a life of its own. Never just a devotion among others, it proved to be a super-devotion unlike any seen before. It was as if the Divine Office, which until then had been the prerogative of religious, was now put within reach of everyone, for by means of the Mysteries and three simple prayers known to all, an entire year was no longer required to carry the devout through the Church's liturgical cycle. The Rosary could complete the history of our Redemption in a week, a day or even an hour! Who could not find time for the *Opusculum Mariae*?

Never at any time restricted to the clergy, the Rosary came to be known as "the layman's breviary." The only devotion to be raised to a liturgical status on a par with that of the Sacred Heart of Jesus, it would eventually be accorded its own feast day on October 7. First inserted into the Roman Martyrology by Clement VII, it was instituted with proper office by Pope Gregory XIII, and later extended to the universal Church by Clement XI. Benedict XIII included the feast in the Breviary, and Leo XIII dedicated the entire month of October to Our Lady of the Holy Rosary.

III.

Apart from the Blessed Virgin the Rosary is an incomprehensible phenomenon. Wrote Fr. James in *The Secret of Holiness*:

> When we speak of Mary as a figure of the Church, as we do, we are prone to speak as if the preeminence belonged to the Church. In reality it is not so. Preeminence belongs rightly to Mary who is the ideal actualized in a living person, and she it is (in her unique relation to Christ) from whom the Church takes life and meaning. It is only when this deep truth is pondered in the light of which Mary is the true prototype and divine ideal of the Church on earth that the real dimensions of the Church are discerned. Mary is already what the Church has yet to be in the fullness of her being.

Venerable Maria de Agreda habitually referred to her as *la divina Maria*. Today theologians in the line of St. Bonaventure and the Franciscan school are beginning to explore the possibility of the pre-existence of her soul before the world was made. Indeed the liturgy of the Church from earliest times has not hesitated to apply to her those beautiful, mysterious texts of Scripture which describe God's wisdom personified, whom "the Lord possessed from the beginning of His ways, before He made anything, from the beginning. From eternity was I established, and of old before the earth was made." She is also that "mother of fair love" whose "abode is in the full assembly of the saints."

Her "overshadowing" by the Holy Ghost which effected our Lord's Incarnation is the closest approximation in creation to an incarnation of the Third Person of the Blessed Trinity. According to St. Maximilian Kolbe, she "is so closely allied with the Holy Ghost that she is called His spouse ... She is, so to speak, the personification of the Holy Ghost! Jesus Christ is the Mediator between God and humanity; the Immaculata is the unique mediatrix between Jesus and humanity.

> Just as Jesus Christ, to show His great love for us, became Man, so too the third Person, God-Who-Is-Love, willed to show His mediation as regards the Father and the Son by means of a concrete sign: this sign is the Heart of the Immaculate Virgin! It remains true to say that Mary's action is the very action of the Holy Ghost ... Let us grasp how impossible it is to separate the Holy Ghost from Mary the Immaculata, since she is the instrument He uses in all He does in the order of grace.

As Mother of Christ and His clergy, her position is incomparably superior to that of Christ's vicar the Pope, whose infallibility is a privilege related to her Immaculate Conception. The liturgy says of her, "They who work by me shall not sin. They that explain me shall have life everlasting."[4] St. Louis de Montfort, probably the greatest Marian apostle of modern times, taught that to address her is to address God himself by the most efficacious means, so closely is she identified with the divinity.

At La Salette, when she complained to the children Melanie and Maximin of the widespread desecration of Sundays, she said, "I have given you six days in which to work. I kept the seventh for myself, and people don't want to give it to me. This is what makes my Son's arm so heavy." Many found this statement shocking. How could she who was so humble say such a thing? Didn't she mean, "*God* gave you six days?" At the time

---

[4] See the Lessons for the Feast of the Immaculate Conception, its Vigil and the Common

the two children were accused of misquoting her, but neither could be induced to change one word of their testimony, then or later. Because some Catholic editors not so scrupulous took it upon themselves to correct the seers in the name of orthodoxy, the bothersome authentic version has since been conveniently forgotten.

The Rosary is the ultimate liturgy. It finds its place as easily in a concentration camp as in church. After the Holy Sacrifice of the Mass and the Sacraments, it is the most powerful weapon ever placed at the disposition of the faithful. Dare we say more powerful? Yes, in the sense that, somewhat like Baptism and Marriage, it does not depend on the clergy—or in fact on any human being. Although not actually a Sacrament, through Mary Mediatrix of All Graces it infallibly opens to us at any time or place the inexhaustible fountain of living water flowing from the Sacred Heart of the Savior.

Were the Mass and the Sacraments to disappear for a time, the miraculous efficacy of the Rosary could not fail to be evident. Pius XII writes:

> From the frequent meditation on the Mysteries the soul draws and imperceptibly absorbs the virtues they contain, and lights up with extraordinary hope of the immortal virtues, and becomes strongly and easily impelled to follow the path which Christ himself and His Mother have followed.

It is possible to pray the Rosary in isolation, but never alone. As an integral part of the liturgy of the Church, it cannot be prayed outside the Communion of Saints. No more powerful "private" prayer exists, for it is the prayer of Christ himself in His Mystical Body. Venerable Pauline Jaricot, foundress of the Propagation of the Faith, established the Association of the Living Rosary as a tool of the apostolate in the shambles following the French Revolution. Encouraged by the Cure d' Ars and invoking the intercession of St. Philomena, she succeeded in reviving the faith of millions by the simple expedient of forming everywhere little groups of fifteen individuals, each of whom was assigned one particular decade to be said daily.

Persons from all walks of life, including the aged and the sick, became missionaries overnight. Not only did the missions benefit, but members of the Association as well. Pauline very wisely did not seek recruits only among the fervent. She found her group Rosary "a way to utilize the strength of these few isolated souls and enable them to share their spiritual vigor with those more spiritually impoverished." It proved "a means for them to inject their spiritual 'remedy' drop by drop into the souls of others as 'spiritual medicine. 'If acknowledging that "it was wise to make the good souls better," She also realized that "this devotion would render spiritual health to those who were languishing."[5]

Leo XIII declared in *Octobri mense*, "We may well believe that the Queen of Heaven herself has granted *a special efficacy to this mode of supplication*." His words would be reaffirmed by Sr. Lucy, the visionary of Fatima, who told Fr. Fuentes:

> The Most Holy Virgin in these last times in which we live has given *a new efficacy* to the recitation of the Rosary, to such an extent that there is no problem, no matter how difficult it is, whether temporal, or above all, spiritual, in the personal life of each one of us, of our families, of the families of the world or of religious communities, or even of the life of peoples and nations that cannot be solved by the Rosary. There is no problem, I tell

---

[5] A heartening revival of Pauline Jaricot's work began in the U.S. in 1986, when the Universal Living Rosary Association was established at Box 1303, Dickinson Texas, 775539 and began soliciting enrollments worldwide. Current membership numbers about 160,000.

you, no matter how difficult it is, that we cannot resolve by the prayer of the Rosary! With the Holy Rosary we will save ourselves. We will sanctify ourselves. We will console our Lord and obtain the salvation of many souls.

To the Italian Salesian Dom Umberto Pasquale she wrote in 1970:

> The decadence which exists in the world is without any doubt the consequence of the lack of the spirit of prayer. Foreseeing this disorientation, the Blessed Virgin recommended recitation of the Rosary with such insistence, and since the Rosary is, after the Eucharistic liturgy, the prayer most apt for preserving faith in souls, the devil has unchained his struggle against it .... The Rosary is the most powerful weapon for defending ourselves on the field of battle.[6]

She writes in the same year to Mother Martins on how,

> ...the devil has succeeded in infiltrating evil under cover of good ... And the worst is that he has succeeded in leading into error and deceiving souls having a heavy responsibility through the place they occupy ... They are blind men guiding other blind men![7]

Against the blunders and injustices committed by legitimate authority, prayer is almost the only recourse open to the ordinary faithful. Let them pray the Rosary day in and day out, over and over. The constant repetition of the prayers and Mysteries, which innovators find monotonous and antiquated, anchors it to the rhythms of God's creation, where the same sun rises every day and the same seasons return every year.

---

[6] Michael de la Sainte Trinité, *The Third Secret*, Immaculate Heart Publications, 1990, p. 759.

[7] *Op. cit.*, p. 758

Where there is no repetition there is chaos, for peace and order in this world cannot exist apart from it. "The recitation of identical formulas repeated so many times," writes Pius XII, "rather than rendering the prayer sterile and boring, has on the contrary the admirable quality of infusing confidence in him who prays and makes a sweet compulsion toward the Immaculate Heart of Mary." To one of her priest nephews Sr. Lucy writes:

> The repetition of the *Ave Maria*, *Pater Noster* and *Gloria Patri* is the chain that lifts us right up to God and unites us to Him, giving us a participation in His divine life, just as eating bite after bite of bread, from which we nourish ourselves, sustains the natural life in us; nobody calls that outdated![8]

Whoever prays the Rosary is formally joined to the prayer of the Church in a most informal way. Proclaiming the everlasting *Sanctus* with every "*Glory be*," the Rosary partakes of the angelic liturgy before the throne of the Lamb eternally immolated in heaven. The persecuted Catholics of Ireland were on sure doctrinal ground when they resorted to the "beads" for a "dry Mass." As our earthly liturgy continues to disintegrate and the ranks of the priesthood to dwindle, this is good to remember. Older Catholics do in fact remember when it was accepted practice to participate in the Holy Sacrifice by saying the Rosary.

In a letter written to another of her priest nephews, Sr. Lucy referred to this method once known to all:

> It is false to say that this is not liturgical, because the prayers of the Rosary are all part of the sacred liturgy; and if they are not displeasing to God when we recite them as we celebrate the Holy Sacrifice, so also they do not displease Him if we recite them in His presence, when He is exposed for our adoration . ... Why would the prayer which God taught us and so much recommended to us be outdated? It is easy to recognize here the ruse of the devil and his followers, who want to lead souls away from God by

---

[8] *Op. cit.,* p. 751

leading them away from prayer ... Do not let yourselves be deceived![9]

IV.

Much as our Lady had set heaven's seal on Pius IX's promulgation of the dogma of the Immaculate Conception by appearing at Lourdes in 1858 and proclaiming, "I am the Immaculate Conception," she would ratify Leo XIII's teachings on the Rosary by appearing at Fatima in 1917 and proclaiming "I am the Lady of the Rosary."

There were six apparitions, in all of which she was seen, as at Lourdes, with the Rosary. During the last one on October 13, while the great miracle of the sun was in progress, Sr. Lucy saw three extraordinary tableaux displayed in the heavens: one of the Holy Family, symbolizing the Joyful Mysteries of the Rosary; a second one of the Mother of Sorrows, symbolizing the Sorrowful Mysteries; and a third one of our Lady crowned and reigning in glory as Our Lady of Mt. Carmel, symbolizing the Glorious Mysteries.

This spectacular testimony to the Rosary was not the first to be deployed in the heavens. Although unknown to the generality of Catholics and now nearly forgotten, a similar one is believed to have occurred twenty years before the spectacle in Fatima at Tilly-sur-Seulles, a little French village in Calvados. According to the account by Guy Le Rumeur, all fifteen mysteries were seen in the sky by a young visionary named Marie Cartel, who had never before heard of them:

> She read there not only their classification as Joyous, Sorrowful and Glorious, but their fruits as well. We know that the local Ordinary, who neither examined nor judged the case of these apparitions, proceeded in such wise that they could not be recognized. ... Nevertheless popular common sense, supported in 1905 by some French and Roman clergy, never rejected these apparitions, and Tilly-sur-Seulles continued to be a place of pilgrimage. A chapel, erected with diocesan approval, was

---

[9] *Op. cit.,* p. 752

destroyed during the battles of 1944 but rebuilt in 1952-3. Marble tablets inscribed with the fifteen mysteries can be found there, which were granted an Imprimatur in 1954.[10]

Four years before the apparitions at Tilly Leo XIII had issued the encyclical *Laetitia sanctae*. Dated on our Lady's birthday 1893, it belongs by right among his social encyclicals, for it proposed a schema for curing the three principal ills of modern society in terms of the Rosary, teaching that,

1. *the distaste for simple labor* which characterizes the industrial age must yield to the salutary precepts of the Joyful Mysteries;

2. *the repugnance for suffering* endemic to a pleasure-motivated society must be overcome by living the Sorrowful Mysteries; and

3. *the lethal forgetfulness of a future life* must be dispelled by ordering all human endeavor to the Glorious Mysteries.

Already in 1884 Leo had warned in *Superiore anno*:

> For it is an arduous and exceedingly weighty matter that is now at hand: to overcome the ancient and insidious enemy, Satan, in the brazen array of his power; to win back the freedom of the Church and of her Head; to preserve and secure the fortifications within which should rest the safety and well being of human society. Care must be taken, therefore, that in these times of mourning for the Church, the most holy Rosary of Mary be assiduously and piously observed, particularly since this method of prayer, being so arranged as to recall in turn all the mysteries of our salvation, is eminently fitted to foster the spirit of piety.

At Fatima our Lady told her children once and for all, "I want you to continue to say the Rosary every day!" A complete Rosary has fifteen decades, and not only five like the chaplet.

---

[10] *Op. cit.,* pp. 19, 211.

Padre Pio is said to have offered a hundred daily. Because it is liturgy placed within the reach of all and enjoined upon all with such insistence by the Mother of God, there is good reason to believe that its recital is not optional in the scheme of salvation. She told Bl. Alan, "Know my son, that a probable and proximate sign of eternal damnation is aversion for, lukewarmness and carelessness in saying the Angelic Salutation which has repaired the whole world!"

As once against the errors of the Cathars, Mary's children are now being told to fling the Rosary against the "errors of Russia" which are drawing the whole world into Satan's eternal fiery empire. In 1957 Sr. Lucy told Fr. Fuentes,

> The Most Holy Virgin made me understand that we are living in the last times of the world. ... She told me that the devil is in the process of engaging in a decisive battle against the Blessed Virgin, and a decisive battle is the final battle where one side will be victorious and the other side will suffer defeat.

Foreseeing these times, St. Louis de Montfort called for,

> ...true servants of the Blessed Virgin who, like so many St. Dominics, would go everywhere, the burning, blazing brand of the Gospel in their mouths and the Holy Rosary in their hands, barking like dogs, burning like fire, dispelling the world's darkness like suns, and who, by means of devotion to Mary ... would crush the head of the ancient serpent wherever they went.[11]

Damaged perspective is quickly corrected by reference to the Mysteries of the Rosary, which contain the whole of human history in prophecy. For the Church there is no possibility of failure. Faithfully reproducing the life of her blessed Lord on earth as Mary did, she has left the Joyful Mysteries far behind and is already at grips with the Sorrowful ones. Approaching her own crucifixion, she is even now on the Way of the Cross which leads to the Resurrection. Like her divine Master, "who having joy set before Him, endured the cross, despising the shame"

---

[11] *Prière Embrasée*, 12

(Heb.12:2), she keeps her gaze fixed on the Glorious Mysteries lying ahead.

Conformed to Him in all things, the Church can expect her torment to end like His, abruptly and without warning, leaving the world to marvel as did Pilate, who "wondered that he should already be dead" *(Mk. 15:44)*. Suffering is suffering because it is not natural to man, who was created to share God's own eternal happiness and glory. The Sacred Heart has promised, "I shall reign in spite of Satan and all opposition!" Revealing her own participation in that promise, His Mother has declared, "In the end my immaculate Heart will triumph." In their one Heart is laid up one inevitable, final resplendent victory.

MARY'S REMNANT

The first Merry Christmas the faithful remnant of Israel had was the first Christmas. Incontrovertible vindication of their harried hopes, our Lord's birth in a stable at Bethlehem promised them even greater vindication in the future. It was only fitting that the angels of heaven and the wise kings of the earth should join them at such a time to celebrate God's glory. Of all people who ever lived, the remnant had most reason to be deliriously, deliciously merry. *Gloria in excelsis Deo!* Peace on earth was promised to them, the men of good will.

By God's grace, the remnant's own immaculate daughter Mary had just borne the Son of God made Man. This means the remnant had, in a very real sense, in the fullness of time, itself produced Him. No theme was dearer to the prophets of Israel than that of the mysterious remnant, and for centuries the remnant had doggedly believed them. Believing to the bitter end in the face of every evidence to the contrary is what the remnant does best. That indeed is its function. Mary excelled at it.

The remnant isn't an elite in the ordinary sense of the word, for anyone at all may enter its ranks. Rich and poor, highborn and low, the talented and the humdrum, the brave and the cowardly find their way into it. Sometimes the remnant is on the winning side, as it was at Lepanto, but mostly it seems to flourish among the losers. Many are quite respectable, but others, like their divine Master, can be "reckoned along the wicked." Who would have suspected that one of the thieves crucified with Him belonged to the remnant, whereas a trusted Apostle called Judas did not?

Given the nature of its work, its numbers tend to be small and sometimes seem to disappear altogether. At the time of the Flood they were only eight, and at the first Pentecost they totaled only a hundred and twenty. In the days of Jezebel the prophet Elias, for all his thundering, was convinced he was the only one left. Expecting to be dispatched momentarily by the priests of

Baal, he had to be reassured by God himself, who told him, "I have left me seven thousand men, that have not bowed the knee to Baal!" *(Rom. 11:15)*. Obviously, the remnant doesn't have to be visible to be there.

Undetectable as they are, their numbers can be plentiful, as they must have been in the heyday of Catholic Christendom. In the Apocalypse they are shown to be very many indeed, "a great multitude which no man could number, of all nations and tribes and peoples and tongues" *(Apo.7:9)*. Not that numbers mean anything. Quoting Isaiah, St Paul tells us, "If the number of the children of Israel be as the sand of the sea, a remnant shall be saved" *(Rom 9:27)*.

Few or many, the remnant will not suffer description. It is no secret society, yet, on this earth none of its members can be identified for sure, not even oneself. We know only that a remnant exists, because God said so, and He promised there would always be one. In the old Vulgate, the terms the prophets used for "remnant" are usually translated *reliquiae* or occasionally *residuum*. Still, it would not do to think of them as leftovers or a residue of some kind. Scripture is aware of these kinds of remnants, and is careful to point out that the remnants of Baal, of sodomites, or those of Anathoth and the Philistines wind up exterminated.

God's remnant is something that remains. When the fury of whatever is attacking the kingdom of God is spent, the remnant, dead or alive, is still at the battlements. When others dribble off in the wrong directions, the remnant continues to face the right way. On that first Christmas when our Lord was born, nobody noticed the remnant, but they were there with the ox and the ass, and they knew exactly where to find the Son of God made flesh. Herod and the high priests did not, although they easily pinpointed the prophecy which told them where He would be.

"Even so then at this present time also," says St. Paul, "there is a remnant saved according to the election of grace" *(Rom. 11:5)*. Its enviable position has not changed to this day. In the heat of mounting apostasy the remnant still knows there's no salvation outside the Church, and except for those still working their way into her ranks, they aren't budging. The remnant also knows that one can commit involuntary sins, that hell is a place, that marriage is indissoluble and that birth control is wrong even when it's called "natural family planning," plus a lot of other things being forgotten or updated. If it does go wrong sometimes, it will find out sooner or later, and muster the humility to admit it.

Impossible as it is to categorize, the remnant is clearly defined in the Apocalypse. In that famous twelfth chapter whose events Sr. Lucy of Fatima says are now unfolding in the world, we are told straight out what the remnant is: It is Mary's. It is "the rest of her seed" *(Apo. 12:17)*, a phrase which the Vulgate renders as *"reliquiis de semine eius."* Whatever its number and aspect may be, that elusive entity is therefore nothing other than the children of the Woman destined from the beginning to crush the head of the ancient serpent.

This explains why St. Grignion de Montfort and so many other saints and doctors of the Church could declare so confidently that devotion to Mary is one of the surest signs of salvation. It is the one distinguishing characteristic which sets the true remnant of Israel apart from others who may look like it in other respects. It marks those who truly "keep the commandments of God, and have the testimony of Jesus Christ," for Mary is the touchstone of the Faith. Not to accept her infallibly reveals the heretic. Because of her, the remnant's life is hell on earth, for from the beginning the infernal dragon "was angry against the woman, and went to make war with the rest of her seed" *(Apo.12:17)*.

Our Lord grew up in the midst of Mary's remnant, where they had taken refuge in the hills of Galilee. Scholars have determined that pervasive reforms had been imposed on Israel some years before His nativity which were not accepted by all in Judea. Presumably these man-made changes in the calendar and the liturgy are what make it so difficult to synchronize some of the events relating to the Last Supper and the Passion as narrated in the Gospels. It may also explain why shortly before His Passion our Lord at first refused to go up to the Feast of Tabernacles only to attend it three days later, at the traditional time. It's evident the remnant wasn't in step with some arbitrary changes made by the ruling establishment, always knowing how and when to disregard the treacherous "traditions of men" for which our Lord reproved the Pharisees. Except for Judas, most of His disciples were found outside Jerusalem.

The libertarian Albert J. Nock once wrote a little essay entitled "Isaiah's Job" which may become an American classic. In it he asks:

> What do we mean by the masses, and what by the remnant? As the word masses is commonly used, it suggests agglomerations of poor and underprivileged people, laboring people, proletarians. But it means nothing like that; it means simply the majority ... The line of differentiation between the masses and the remnant is set invariably by quality, not by circumstance.

Our Lord never addressed the masses. If He seemed to in the crowds lining the roads of Palestine, He was only seeking His remnant, those His Father had given Him, who "shall not perish forever" and whom "no one shall pluck ... out of my hand!" *(John 10:29-30)*. Regarding the Syro-Phoenician woman seeking a cure for her daughter, He told His disciples, "I was not sent but to the sheep that are lost of the house of Israel" *(Matt. 15:24)*. Missionary effort cannot be directed to the masses, but only to the remnant who will perpetuate that effort. They are a mystery of predestination.

A million or a handful, only they will ever be faithful to the end. When the long-awaited conversion of the Jews occurs, we can be sure it will be no mass return of organized Zionism to the sheepfold, but only the remnant prophesied in Scripture. If we could identify them, we could see some of them now, already on the road. And we could find Zionists among them. Not for the masses of the world does the Son of God pray *(John 17:9)*, but for those who are Mary's, because the world is incapable of receiving the truth *(John 14:17)*. Even as that world dissolves and coagulates into the new man made order of triumphal revolution, the remnant has every reason to be merry.

However their numbers swell, they are always our Lord's "little flock," to whom He attends personally, whispering through His Holy Ghost, "Fear not, for it has pleased your Father to give you a kingdom" *(Luke 12:32)*. "Scattered and driven away" by evil pastors, they feed upon His promise: "I will gather together the remnant of my flock, out of all the lands into which I have cast them out, and I will make them return to their own fields, and they shall be increased and multiplied ... and none shall be wanting of their number" *(Jer. 23:2-4)*. Whoever they are, wherever they are, and whatever they may look like, the remnant has absolutely nothing to worry about. They know exactly where their leadership lies. Now, as at that first Christmas when angels sang on earth, it is where wise men always find Christ the King: "with Mary His mother" *(Matt. 2:11)*.

Hail, Mary, full of grace, the Lord is with thee!

APPENDICES

HAURIETIS AQUAS

ENCYCLICAL OF POPE PIUS XII
ON DEVOTION TO THE SACRED HEART
MAY 15,1956

To Our Venerable Brethren, the Patriarchs, Primates, Archbishops, Bishops and other Local Ordinaries in peace and communion with the Apostolic See:

Health and Apostolic Benediction.

"You shall draw waters with joy out of the Saviour's fountains" *(Is.12,3)*. These words, in which the Prophet Isaias symbolically foretold the manifold and rich gifts of God that Christianity was to reap, spontaneously come to Our mind as We recall the centenary of the proclamation in which Our predecessor of immortal memory, Pius IX, gladly granting the petition of the Catholic world, ordered the celebration of the feast of the Sacred Heart throughout the whole Church.

2. Those heavenly blessings which devotion to the Sacred Heart of Jesus pours into the souls of the faithful, purifying them, refreshing them with heavenly consolation and urging them to acquire all virtues, cannot be counted. Mindful, therefore, of the wise words of the Apostle St. James—"Every good gift and every perfect gift is from above, coming down from the Father of Lights" *(Jas.1,17)*—We rightly see in this devotion, which everywhere grows more fervent, the inestimable gift which the Incarnate Word, our Divine Saviour, as the sole Mediator of grace and truth between the Heavenly Father and the human race, gave to the Church, His mystical bride, in recent times so that she could endure great trials and surmount

difficulties. In virtue of this inestimable gift the Church is able to manifest her ardent love for her Divine Founder and in a fuller measure carry out the injunction given by Jesus Christ Himself, which St. John the Evangelist records: "Now on the last, the great day of the feast, Jesus stood and cried out, saying, 'If anyone thirst, let him come to me and drink. He who believes in me, as the Scripture says, "From within him there shall flow rivers of living water."' He said this, however, of the Spirit whom they who believed in him were to receive" *(Jn.7,37-39).*

3. It was certainly not hard for those who heard Jesus speak these words, in which He promised that a fountain of "living water" would flow from within Him, to recall the words of the holy prophets Isaias, Ezechiel and Zachary foretelling the messianic kingdom, and that rock from which water miraculously gushed forth when Moses struck it. *(Cf.Is.12,3; Ez.47,1-12; Za.13,1; Ex.17,1-7; Nm.20,7-13; I Cor 10,4; Ap.7,17;22,1).*

4. Divine love has its origin in the Holy Ghost, who is the Personified Love both of the Father and the Son in the bosom of the August Trinity. Most aptly, then, does the Apostle of the Gentiles, echoing the words of Jesus Christ, attribute the infusion of charity in the souls of the faithful to this Spirit of Love. "The charity of God is poured forth in our hearts by the Holy Spirit who has been given to us"*(Rom.5,5).*

5. This intimate bond which, according to Sacred Scripture, exists between the divine charity that must burn in the souls of the faithful and the Holy Ghost, clearly shows to all, venerable brothers, the real nature of devotion to the Sacred Heart of Jesus Christ. For it is perfectly clear that this devotion, if we examine its proper nature, is a most excellent act of religion.

6. It demands the full and absolute determination of surrendering and consecrating oneself to the love of the Divine Redeemer. The wounded heart of the Saviour is the living sign and symbol of that love. It is likewise clear, even to a greater

degree, that this devotion especially declares that we must repay divine love with our own love.

7. Indeed it flows from the very essence of love that the souls of men fully and completely submit to the rule of the Supreme Being, because the act of our love so depends upon the divine will that it forms, as it were, a certain oneness according to the words of Scripture, "He who cleaves to the Lord is one in spirit with Him" *(1 Cor.6,17)*.

I

8. The Church has always held devotion to the Sacred Heart of Jesus in such high regard and continues to esteem it so greatly that she strives to have this devotion flourish throughout the world and to promote it in every way. At the same time she is vigilant to safeguard it with all her strength against the charges of naturalism and so-called sentimentalism. In spite of this vigilance, it is nevertheless a deplorable fact that in the past and in our own time this most noble devotion has not even been held in the honor it deserves by some Christians, and at times even by those who claim to be animated by zeal for the Catholic religion and the acquiring of sanctity.

9. "If thou didst know the gift of God"*(Jn.4,10)*, venerable brothers, We, who by the hidden designs of God have been chosen as guardian and dispenser of that sacred treasure of faith and piety which the Divine Redeemer entrusted to His Church, make these words Our own. Through them, in keeping with the duty of Our office, We admonish all those of Our sons who are still led by preconceived opinions, and go so far at times as to consider devotion to the Sacred Heart of Jesus (which triumphing, as it were, over the errors and neglect of men has spread over His whole Mystical Body) as less suited—not to say detrimental—to the more pressing spiritual needs of the Church and the human race in our times.

10. There are some who join the very essence of this devotion with other forms of piety which the Church approves and encourages but does not command. They put it on an equal footing with those other forms of piety. They look upon this devotion as some kind of additive which each one is free to use according to his own good pleasure.

11. There are others, again, who assert that this devotion is burdensome and of little or no use, particularly to those who are fighting in the kingdom of God motivated by the idea of defending, teaching and spreading Catholic truth to the utmost of their strength, resources and time, and of inculcating Christian social teaching and who strive to promote those acts of religion and undertakings which they consider much more necessary today. Then, too, there are those who, far from considering this devotion a powerful help for correctly forming and restoring Christian morals both in the private life of individuals and in the family circle, consider it rather as a form of piety springing from emotions and not from reasoned convictions and more suited, therefore, for women, because they see in it something unbecoming educated men.

12. Others again, when they pause to think that this devotion especially demands penance, expiation and the rest of the virtues which they call passive and which have no external influence, do not consider it apt for arousing the spiritual fervor of our times. Fervor today must aim rather at visible strenuous action, the triumph of the Catholic faith and a vigorous defense of Christian moral standards.

13. As everyone knows these norms are flippantly attacked by the captious objections of those who are indifferent to all religion, who tear down the distinction of true and false in thought and action and who are pitifully contaminated by the principles of atheistic materialism and laicism.

14. Venerable brothers, who does not see that such opinions are completely contrary to the teachings which Our predecessors

publicly proclaimed from this chair of truth when they approved the devotion to the Sacred Heart of Jesus? Who would dare call useless and less suitable to our time that piety which Our predecessor of immortal memory, Leo XIII, declared a "most excellent form of religion" and in which he had no doubt there was to be found a powerful remedy to cure those very same evils which today, too—beyond doubt in an even greater and more violent manner—afflict and vex individuals and society? "This devotion," he said, "which We recommend to all, will be profitable for all."

15. He added these admonitions and exhortations which also apply to devotion to the Sacred Heart of Jesus: "Hence this force of evils, which so long weighs us down seriously, demands that the help of One be sought by whose power it can be driven off. Who is He, but the only begotten Son of God! For there is no other name under heaven given to men by which we must be saved. We must then flee to Him, who is the Way, the Truth and the Life." (Encycl. *Annum Sacrum*, May 25, 1899: A.L., Vol. 19, 1900, pp.71,77-78).

16. Neither did Our immediate predecessor of happy memory, Pius XI, declare this devotion less approved. and suited to foster Christian piety. In an encyclical letter he wrote: "Is not the epitome of religion, and consequently the norm of the more perfect life, contained in that form of piety which more readily leads souls to acknowledge Christ the Lord and which more effectively inclines hearts to love Him more ardently and imitate Him more closely?" (Encycl. *Miserentissimus Redemptor*, May 8,1928: A.A.S.,20, 1928, p.167).

17. This truth is as evident and clear to Us as it was to Our predecessors. When We became Pope and saw with pleasure that devotion to the Sacred Heart of Jesus had providentially increased among Christian peoples and was marching in triumph, so to speak, We were filled with joy at the graces which flowed to the Church from this devotion. We were pleased to note this in Our very first encyclical. (Cfr. Encycl. *Summi Pontificatus*, October 20, 1939:A.A.S.31,1939,p.415).

18. Through the years of Our pontificate, filled not only with cares and anxieties but also with ineffable consolations, these blessings have not been diminished either in number, power or splendor, but have rather been multiplied. Various movements have providentially started which are conducive to the adding of new fervor to this devotion and most aptly suited to the needs of our times. We mean organizations to promote religion and charity, published articles which explain the historical, the ascetical or the mystical aspects which have bearing on this topic and pious works of expiation.

19. We mention especially the proofs of deepest piety given by the Apostleship of Prayer, under whose auspices and care homes, colleges, institutions and at times whole nations were consecrated to the most Sacred Heart of Jesus. Not infrequently by letter, public addresses, and even by radio We have extended Our paternal congratulations to these undertakings." (Cfr. A.A.S. 32, 1940, P.276; 35, 1943, p.470; 37, 1945, pp.263-264; 40, 1948, p.501; 41, 1949, p.331).

20. Consequently, as We behold the rich abundance of salutary waters, that is, of heavenly gifts of divine love, flowing from the Sacred Heart of Our Redeemer and permeating countless children of the Catholic Church (under the inspiration and operation of the Holy Ghost), We cannot refrain, venerable brothers, from exhorting you paternally to join Us in giving glory and thanks to God, the Giver of all good gifts. We join Our sentiments with those of the Apostle of the Gentiles: "Now, to him who is able to accomplish all things in a measure far beyond what we ask to conceive, in keeping with the power that is at work in us—to him be glory in the Church and in Christ Jesus down through all the ages of time without end. Amen" *(Eph.3,20-21).*

21. But after We have duly thanked the Eternal God, We wish through this encyclical to urge you, and all Our dearly beloved children of the Church, to study diligently the teachings of Scripture, the Fathers and theologians—the solid foundation on which devotion to the Sacred Heart of Jesus rests.

22. For we are firmly convinced that only when we have thoroughly investigated the basic and profound nature of this devotion in the light of divinely revealed truth, only then, do We say, can we rightly and fully appreciate its incomparable excellence and its inexhaustible store of heavenly gifts. Only after piously meditating on the countless blessings flowing from this devotion can we worthily celebrate the first centenary of the feast of the most Sacred Heart of Jesus.

23. To give to the minds of the faithful a salutary teaching by virtue of which they can more easily and fully understand the true nature of this devotion and reap its abundant fruits, We shall explain those passages of the Old and New Testaments in which God's infinite love for mankind is revealed and set before us. We can, of course, never really study that love sufficiently. We shall then touch upon the chief points of the teaching of the Fathers and Doctors of the Church.

24. Finally, We shall show in its true light the close connection that exists between the kind of devotion to be shown to the heart of the Divine Redeemer and the veneration due to His love and the love of the August Trinity for all men. For We think that if the principal reasons for this noblest form of piety and the foundations on which it rests are set forth in the light of Scripture and the teaching handed down in the Church, the faithful can more easily "draw waters with joy out of the Saviour's fountains" *(Is.12,3)*.

25. To draw this water means to consider more fully the special importance which devotion to the Sacred Heart of Jesus has in the liturgy of the Church and in her internal and external life and activity, and to have the power to gather those spiritual fruits through which individuals can renew their spiritual life, as the shepherds of the flock of Christ desire. That everyone may be able to understand more fully the doctrine which the passages to be cited from the Old and New Testament proclaim in regard to this devotion, they must above all clearly understand the reason why the Church adores the heart of the Divine Redeemer.

26. Now it is perfectly clear to you, venerable brothers, that there is a twofold reason. The first reason, which also applies to the rest of the most holy members of the body of Jesus Christ, rests on the teaching by which we know that His Heart, as the noblest part of human nature, is hypostatically united to the person of the Divine Word and must therefore be adored in the same way in which the Church adores the Person of the Incarnate Son of God. We deal here with an article of Catholic faith since this point was already solemnly defined in the general Council of Ephesus and the second Council of Constantinople. (Council of Ephesus, Can.8; cfr. Mansi, *Sacrorum Conciliorum Ampliss. Collectio*, 4, 1083 C; Second Council of Constantinople, Can.9; cfr. *Ibid*. 9, 382 E.)

27. The second reason, which refers specifically to the Heart of the Divine Redeemer and in a special manner demands adoration, stems from the fact that His Heart, more than all the rest of the members of His body, is the natural sign and symbol of His boundless love for the human race. Our predecessor of immortal memory, Leo XIII, remarked: "In the Sacred Heart there is the symbol and the express image of the infinite love of Jesus Christ which moves us to love in return." (Cfr. Encycl. *Annum Sacrum*: A.L., Vol.19, 1900, p.76).

28. There is no doubt that Scripture never makes express mention of special veneration paid to the physical heart of the Incarnate Word as the symbol of His most ardent love. If we must openly admit this, it cannot surprise Us nor in any way lead Us to doubt the divine love for us which is the principal reason for this devotion. This love is proclaimed and inculcated both in the Old and New Testaments in such vivid images as to greatly stir our souls. At times these images were presented in the Scripture which announced the coming of the Son of God made man. They can therefore be considered as the beginning of the sign and symbol of that divine love, that is of the most Sacred and Adorable Heart of the Divine Redeemer.

29. For our present purpose we do not consider it necessary to cite many passages from the Old Testament, which contains

truths revealed by God long ago. We deem it sufficient to recall the covenant made between God and the Jewish people which was ratified with peace offerings.

30. Moses wrote the laws of the covenant on two tables of stone and the prophets expounded them. (Cfr. *Ex. 34,27-28*). The covenant was sealed not only by the bonds of God's supreme dominion and the obedience which men owe Him, but was also strengthened and sustained by higher considerations of love.

31. For to the people of Israel the weightiest reason for obeying God was not the fear of divine vengeance, which the thunder and lightning flashing from the peak of Mt. Sinai struck into their souls, but rather love for God. "Hear, O Israel! The Lord is our God, the Lord alone! Therefore, you shall love the Lord, your God, with all your heart, and with all your soul, and with all your strength. Take to heart these words which I enjoin on you today" *(Dt. 6,4-6)*.

32. We are not surprised then if Moses and the prophets, whom the Angelic Doctor rightly calls the elders of the chosen people *(Sum. Theol.,* II-II, q.2, a.7: Ed. Leon. tom. 8, 1895, p.34), because they know that the foundation of the entire law was placed on this precept of love, described the dealings between God and his people in terms of the mutual love of a father and his children or of a husband and his wife, rather than in stern terms of God's supreme dominion or of our own subjection in fear.

33. Therefore, to cite a few examples, Moses himself, when he sang his famous canticle because of the liberation of his people from the bondage of Egypt and wanted to declare that it had been accomplished by the power of God, used these touching expressions and comparisons: "As an eagle incites its nestlings forth by hovering over its brood, so he (God) spread his wings to receive them and bore them up on his pinions" *(Dt. 32,11)*.

34. Of the prophets perhaps none more than Osee expresses and explains so clearly and forcefully the love which God always showed His people. In the writings of this prophet, which is outstanding among the rest of the minor prophets for the austere grandeur of his diction, God manifests a holy and solicitous love for His chosen people, a love like that of a loving and merciful father or that of a husband whose honor is offended.

35. It is a question here of a love that is so far from diminishing or ceasing on account of the perfidy of traitors or enormous crimes, that it will rather justly punish offenses, not indeed to repudiate and dismiss the estranged and faithless wife and ungrateful children, but to make amends and purify and reunite them in renewed and strengthened bonds of love. "Because Israel was a child and I loved him; and I called my son out of Egypt ... And I was like a foster father to Ephraim, I carried them in my arms; and they knew not that I healed them. I will draw them with the cords of Adam, with the bands of love ... I will heal their breaches, I will love them freely, for my wrath is turned away from them. I will be as the dew, Israel shall spring as the lily, and his root shall shoot forth as that of Libanus" *(Os. 11,1,3-4;14,5-6).*

36. The prophet Isaias expresses similar sentiments when he represents God Himself and His chosen people expressing, as it were, opposite views in a conversation: "And Sion said: The Lord hath forsaken me, and the Lord hath forgotten me. Can a woman forget her infant, so as not to have pity on the son of her womb? And if she should forget, yet will not I forget thee" *(Is.49,14-15).*

37. No less touching are the words which the author of the Canticle of Canticles uses when he graphically describes the bonds of mutual love which join God and His chosen people in terms of conjugal love. "As a lily among thorns, so is my beloved among women ... My lover belongs to me and I to him; he browses among the lilies ... Set me as a seal on your heart, as a seal on your arm; for stern as death is love, relentless as the

nether world is devotion; its flames are a blazing fire *(Ct. 2,2; 6,3 8,6)*.

38. Yet this most tender, indulgent and patient love of God, which indeed disclaimed the Jewish people as it added crime upon crime, yet never completely repudiated it, and which seems ardent indeed and sublime, was but a harbinger of the most ardent love which the promised Redeemer was to unfold for all from His Most Loving Heart. This love, was to be the exemplar of our love, the foundation of the new covenant. However, only He who is the only Begotten of the Father and the Word-made-Flesh "full of grace and of truth" *(Jn.I,14)* when He came among men weighed down with countless sins and miseries could in His human nature, hypostatically united with the Divine Person, open for mankind "a fountain of living water" to irrigate the parched earth and transform it into a blooming fruitful garden.

39. It seems that the prophet Jeremias in a way foretold this marvelous transformation to be accomplished through God's most merciful and eternal love in these words: "I have loved thee with an everlasting love, therefore have I drawn thee, taking pity on thee ... Behold the days shall come, saith the Lord, and I will make a new covenant with the house of Israel, and with the house of Juda ... This shall be the covenant that I will make with the house of Israel, after those days, saith the Lord: I will give my law in their bowels, and I will write it in their heart, and I will be their God, and they shall be my people ... for I will forgive their iniquity, and I will remember their sin no more" *(Jer.31 ,3;31,33-34)*.

II

40. However, only from the Gospels do we get clear and full knowledge of the new covenant between God and man. The covenant which Moses made between the people of Israel and God was merely the symbol and token which the prophet Jeremias foretold. The real new covenant, We say, is that which was established and accomplished by the Incarnate Word and

divine grace reconciling us with God. This covenant must therefore be considered incomparably nobler and more lasting because it was ratified, not by the blood of goats and heifers, as was the first, but by His Most Holy Blood, which the peace offerings —irrational animals—foreshadowed as "the lamb of God, who takes away the sin of the world." (Cf.*Jn.1,29; Hebr.9,18-28;10,1-17.*)

41. The Christian covenant, much more than the old covenant, clearly shows that it was not based on submission and fear, but ratified in terms of that friendship that must exist between a father and his sons and is sustained and strengthened by a more lavish participation in divine grace and truth, according to the words of St. John the Evangelist: "And of his fullness we have all received, grace for grace. For the Law was given through Moses; grace and truth came through Jesus Christ" *(Jn.1,16-17)*.

42. Since we are led then to the very mystery of the infinite love of the Incarnate Word by the statement of that disciple "whom Jesus loved, the one who, at the supper, had leaned back upon his breast" *(Jn.21,20)*, it seems meet and just, right and availing unto salvation, venerable brothers, to linger awhile in the sweetest contemplation of that mystery.

43. We pause in this consideration so that, enlightened by that light which shines from the Gospel and sheds light on this mystery, We too may conceive and express the desire recorded by the Apostle of the Gentiles: "To have Christ dwelling through faith in your hearts: so that, being rooted and grounded in love, you may be able to comprehend with all the saints what is its breadth and length and height and depth, and to know Christ's love which surpasses knowledge, in order that you may be filled unto all the fullness of God" *(Eph.3,17-19)*.

44. The mystery of the divine Redemption is first and foremost a mystery of love, that is, of the true love of Christ for His Heavenly Father, to whom the sacrifice offered on the Cross

in loving obedience renders most abundant and infinite satisfactions for the sins of mankind. "By suffering out of love and obedience, Christ gave more to God than was required to compensate for the offense of the whole human race" (*Sum. Theol.* 3, q.48, a2; Ed. Leon. tom. 11,1903, p.464). It is, moreover, a mystery of the merciful love of the August Trinity and the Divine Redeemer for all mankind. Since men could in no way expiate their sins (cfr. Encycl. *Miserentissimus Redemptor*, A.A.S.20, 1928,p. 170), Christ through the incalculable riches of His merits which He acquired for us by shedding His precious Blood, was able to restore and perfect the bond of friendship between God and men which had been severed first in Paradise by the pitiful fall of Adam, and later by the countless sins of the chosen people.

45. Therefore the Divine Redeemer, as our duly constituted and perfect Mediator, because He made perfect satisfaction to divine justice for all the debts and obligations of the human race out of His most ardent love for us, effected the marvelous reconciliation between divine justice and divine mercy which constitutes the impenetrable mystery of our salvation.

46. Concerning this mystery, the Angelic Doctor wisely says: "That man should be delivered by Christ's Passion was in keeping with both His mercy and His justice. With His justice, because by His passion Christ made satisfaction for the sin of the human race; and so that man was set free by Christ's justice; and with His mercy, for since man of himself could not satisfy for the sin of all human nature God gave him His Son to satisfy for him.

47. "And this came of a more copious mercy than if He had forgiven sins without satisfaction. Hence St. Paul says: 'God, Who is rich in mercy, by reason of His very great love wherewith He has loved us even when we were dead by reason of our sins, brought us to life together with Christ'" (*Eph. 2,4; Sum. Theol.* 3, q.46, a.1 ad 3; Ed. Leon. tom. 11, 1903, p.436).

48. However, that we may be able so far as it is possible for mortal man "to comprehend with all the saints what is the breadth and length and height and depth" *(Eph.3,18)* of the fathomless love of the Incarnate Word for His Heavenly Father and for men defiled by sin, we must understand that His love was spiritual, as becomes God, because "God is spirit" *(Jn.4-24)*. But it was not only spiritual. To be sure, the love with which God loved our first parents and the Hebrew people was of a spiritual nature. The expressions of love, so human, intimate and paternal which we read in the psalms, in the writings of the prophets and in the Canticle of Canticles, are indications and manifestations of the truest but entirely spiritual love with which God loved the human race. On the contrary, the love spoken of in the Gospel, the letters of the apostles and the pages of the Apocalypse—all of which describe the love of the heart of Jesus Christ—express not only divine love but also human sentiments of love.

49. This point is quite clear to all who are Catholics. For the Word of God assumed not a fictitious and empty body, as some heretics already maintained in the first century of the Christian era and who were condemned by St. John the Apostle in most severe terms: "For many deceivers have gone forth into the world, who do not confess Jesus as the Christ coming in the flesh. This is the deceiver and the Antichrist" *(2 Jn. 7)*. But the Word actually united to His divine person an individual, integral and perfect human nature which was conceived by the power of the Holy Ghost in the most pure womb of the Virgin Mary. (cfr. *Lk. 1,35*). Nothing, therefore, was lacking in the human nature which the Word of God joined to Himself. Indeed He assumed a human nature in no way diminished or changed in its spiritual and bodily capacities, that is, a nature endowed with intelligence and free will and the rest of the internal and external faculties of perception, sense appetites and all natural impulses.

50. The Catholic Church teaches all these doctrines as solemnly proclaimed and confirmed by the Roman Pontiffs and general councils. "Whole and entire in what is His own, whole

and entire in what is ours." (St. Leo the Great, *Epist, Dogm. "Lectis dilectionis tuae" ad Flavianum Canst. Patr.*13 June, a.449; cfr.P.L.54, 763.) "Perfect in His Godhead and likewise perfect in His Humanity" (Council of Chalcedon, a.451; cfr. Mansi. *Op.Cit.* 7,115 B). "Complete God is man, complete man is God." (Pope St. Gelasius, Tract 3: *"Necessarium" Of the Two Natures in Christ,* cfr. A Thiel, *Letters of the Roman Pontiffs from St. Hilary to Pelagius II*, p. 532).

51. Therefore, there can be no doubt that Jesus Christ took a human body having all the affections which are proper to it, along which love holds the first place. There can likewise be no doubt that He had a physical heart like ours, since without this most excellent organ human life, even as regards affections, is impossible. Wherefore, the heart of Jesus Christ, hypostatically united to the Divine Person of the Word, beyond doubt throbbed with love and the rest of the impulses of the affections which, however, were in such perfect accord and harmony with His human will filled with divine love and the infinite love itself which the Son shares with the Father and the Holy Ghost so that there never was anything contrary or conflicting in these three kinds of love. (Cfr. St. Thomas *Sum. Theol.*3, q.15, a 4; q.18, a.6; Ed. Leon. tom. 11, 1903, p.189 and 237).

52. Nevertheless, We say that the Word of God took upon Himself a "real" and perfect human nature and formed and fashioned for Himself a heart of flesh, which, like ours could suffer and be pierced. We repeat that unless this teaching be considered not only in the light which is shed by the hypostatic and substantial union, but also in that of the redemption of mankind—its complement, as it were—this doctrine can be a stumbling block and foolishness to some, as Christ nailed to the Cross actually was to the Jews and Gentiles. *(Cfr. 1 Cor. 1,23).*

53. The authoritative teaching of the Catholic faith, since it is in complete agreement with Scripture, assures us that the only begotten Son of God assumed a human nature capable of suffering and dying precisely because He wished, by offering the

bloody sacrifice on the Cross, to accomplish the task of man's redemption.

54. For the rest, the Apostle of the Gentiles teaches this doctrine in these words: "For both he who sanctifies and they who are sanctified are all from one. For which cause he is not ashamed to call them brethren, saying, 'I will declare thy name to my brethren' ... And again, 'Behold I and my children, whom God has given me.' Therefore, because children have blood and flesh in common, so he in like manner has shared in these ... Wherefore it was right that he should in all things be made like unto his brethren, that he might become a merciful and faithful high priest before God to expiate the sins of the people. For in that he himself has suffered and has been tempted, he is able to help those who are tempted" *(Heb. 2, 11-14; 17-18).*

55. The Fathers of the Church, truthful witnesses of divinely revealed doctrine, understood most definitely what the Apostle Paul has quite clearly stated: that the mysteries of the Incarnation and Redemption were the beginning and culmination of divine love. Frequently, and in clear words, we read in their writings that Jesus Christ assumed perfect human nature, and our mortal and perishable body, to provide for our eternal salvation and to show us His infinite, even sensible love.

56. Echoing the words of the Apostle of the Gentiles, St. Justin writes: "We adore and love the Word born of the unbegotten and ineffable God since He became Man for our sake, so that having become partaker of our sufferings He might provide a remedy for them." *(Apol. 2,13; P.G.6, 465).* St. Basil, the greatest of the three Cappadocian Fathers, teaches that the affections of the senses in Christ were at one and the same time real and holy. "It is clear that the Lord indeed did assume natural affections as a proof of His real and not imaginary Incarnation and that He rejected as unworthy of the Godhead corrupt affections which defile the purity of our life. " (Epist. 261,3; P.G.32, 972). In like manner the light of the church of Antioch, St. John Chrysostom, states that the affections of the senses to which the

Divine Redeemer was susceptible prove beyond doubt that He assumed a complete human nature. "For if He had not shared our nature He would not have repeatedly been seized with grief." (In Joann. Homil. 63,2; P.G. 50, 350).

57. Of the Latin Fathers We select for mention those whom the Church today honors as the greatest. St. Ambrose testifies that the movements of the senses and the affections, from which the Incarnate Word was not free, are rooted in the hypostatic union as in a natural principle: "And therefore he assumed a soul and the passions of the soul; for God precisely because He is God could not have been disturbed nor could He have died." (*De fide ad Gratianum*, 2, 7,56; P.L. 16, 594).

58. From these affections St. Jerome draws his chief proof that Christ assumed human nature: "To prove that He really assumed human nature, he really became sorrowful." (*Super Matth.* 26, 37; P.L. 26, 205). St. Augustine in a special manner calls attention to the relations between the affections of the Incarnate Word and the purpose of the redemption of the human race. "These affections of human infirmity, just as the human body itself and death, the Lord Jesus assumed not out of necessity but freely out of compassion so that He might transform in Himself His body, which is the Church of which He deigned to be the Head, that is, His members who are among the faithful and the saints so that if any of them in trials of this life should be saddened and afflicted, they should not therefore think that they are deprived of His grace; nor should they consider this sorrow a sin, but a sign of human weakness; like a choir singing in harmony with the note that has been sounded, so should his body learn from its Head." (*Enarr.in Ps.* 87,3; P.L. 37,1111).

59. In less ornate but nevertheless forceful words, the following passages from St. John Damascene set forth the clear teaching of the Church: "Complete God assumed complete man, and complete man is united to complete God so that He might bring salvation to complete man. For what was not assumed

could not be healed." (*De Fide Orth*.3,6: P.G. 94, 1006). "He therefore assumed all that He might sanctify all." (*Ibid.* 3,20: P.G. 94, 1801).

60. We must, however, bear in mind that these quotations from scripture and the Fathers and not a few similar ones which We did not cite, although they clearly attest that there were in Jesus Christ movements of the senses and affections and that he assumed human nature to accomplish our eternal salvation, they never refer to His physical heart in such a manner as to clearly indicate it as the symbol of His infinite love.

61. But if the evangelists and the rest of the sacred writers do not clearly describe the heart of our Redeemer as responding to feelings and emotions no less than ours and as throbbing and palpitating on account of the various movements and affections of his soul and of the most ardent love of His human and divine wills, they do frequently, however, clearly record His divine love and those movements of the emotions connected with them, namely, desire, joy, sadness, fear and anger as they are reflected in His countenance, words and manner of acting.

62. The countenance of our adorable Saviour was an indication and perfect mirror of those affections which, in various ways, moved His soul, and of the reactions which reached and touched His Most Sacred Heart. The observation based on common experience which the Angelic Doctor made concerning human psychology and what follows from it is pertinent to this matter: "The disturbance of anger reaches to the outward members and chiefly to those members which reflect more distinctly the emotions of the heart, such as the eyes, face and tongue." (*Sum. Theol.* 1-2, q. 48, a.4; Ed. Leon. tom. 6, 1891, p.306).

63. Wherefore the heart of the Incarnate Word is rightly considered the chief index and symbol of the threefold love with which the Divine Redeemer continuously loves the Eternal Father and the Whole human race. It is the symbol of that divine love which He shares with the Father and the Holy Ghost, but which in Him alone, in the Word namely that was made Flesh, is

it manifested to us through His mortal human body, since "in Him dwells the fullness of the Godhead bodily" *(Col. 2,9)*.

64. It is moreover the symbol of that most ardent love which, infused into His soul, sanctifies the human will of Christ and whose action is enlightened and directed by a twofold most perfect knowledge, namely the beatific and infused." (Cfr. *Sum. Theol.*,3, q.9, a.1-3: Ed. Leon. tom. 11, 1903, p.142).

65. Finally, in a more direct and natural manner, it is a symbol also of sensible love, since the body of Jesus Christ, formed through the operation of the Holy Ghost in the womb of the Virgin Mary, has a most perfect capacity for feeling and perception, much more than the bodies of all other men. (Cfr. *Ibid.* 3, q.33, a.2, ad 3m; q.46, a.6: Ed. Leon. tom. 11, 1903, pp. 342,433).

66. Since Scripture and the teachings of the Catholic Faith affirm that there is the highest possible harmony and agreement in the Most Holy Soul of Jesus Christ, and that He clearly directed His threefold love to accomplish our redemption, it is therefore obvious that we can most correctly consider and venerate the heart of the Divine Redeemer as signifying the image of His love, the proof of our redemption and the mystical ladder by which we climb to the embrace of "God our Saviour" *(Tit. 3,4)*.

67. Wherefore His words, actions, teachings, miracles, and in particular those deeds which more clearly testify this love for us—the institution of the Holy Eucharist, His most bitter passion and death, His Most Holy Mother whom He lovingly gave to us, the founding of the Church and the sending of the Holy Ghost upon the apostles and upon us—all these we must regard as proofs of His threefold love.

68. In like manner we must lovingly meditate on the pulsations of His most Sacred Heart by which, so to say, He Himself kept on measuring the time of His sojourn on earth up to the last moment when, as evangelists testify "crying out in a loud

voice 'It is consummated,' and, bowing his head, gave up His spirit" *(Mt. 27,50, Jn. 19,30)*.

69. Then the beating of His heart stopped, and His sensible love was interrupted until He arose from the tomb in triumph over death.

70. But after His glorified body was again united to the soul of the Divine Redeemer, the Conqueror of death, His Most Sacred Heart never ceased, and never will cease, to beat with imperturbable and calm pulsation. It will likewise never cease to signify His threefold love by which the Son of God is bound to His heavenly Father and the whole human race, of which He is by perfect right the mystical head.

III

71. But now, venerable brothers, in order that we may gather rich and salutary fruits from these considerations, let us briefly meditate on and contemplate the manifold affections, human and divine, of Our Saviour, Jesus Christ. These indeed His Heart manifested through the course of His mortal life.

72. These affections He now manifests and will continue to do so forever. Especially from the pages of the Gospel does light shine forth to us. Illumined and strengthened by this light, we can enter into the tabernacle of His Divine Heart. Together with the Apostle of the Gentiles we can wonder at "the riches of grace in kindness towards us in Christ Jesus" *(Eph. 2,7)*.

73. The adorable Heart of Jesus Christ beats with human and divine love since the Virgin Mary pronounced that great-souled "Fiat" and the Word of God, as the Apostle observes, coming into the world, he says, "Sacrifice and oblation thou wouldst not, but a body thou has fitted to me: in holocausts and sin-offerings thou hast had no pleasure. Then said I, 'Behold, I come'! ... It is in this 'will' that we have been sanctified through the offering of the body of Jesus Christ once for all." *(Heb.10,5-7,10)*.

74. In the same way was He moved by love in perfect accord with the affections of His human will and divine love when in the home at Nazareth He engaged in heavenly discourse with His most sweet Mother and with His foster-father, Joseph. He was obedient to him and He toiled with him in the carpenter's trade and, with the triple love of which We have spoken, He was driven on during the lengthy apostolic journeys which He undertook, in the innumerable miracles which He wrought and by which He recalled the dead from the tomb or bestowed health on those ill with every sort of disease. He was moved by this triple love during the labors He endured, in the sweat, hunger and thirst He suffered and in the nocturnal vigils in which He most lovingly prayed to His Heavenly Father.

75. And finally He was moved by this triple love in the discourses He held and in the parables which He spoke and explained. This is especially true of the parables which treat of His mercy, such as those which tell of the lost drachma, the lost sheep, the prodigal son. In these parables, both by their subject matter and by words, the very Heart of God is expressly laid bare to us, as Gregory the Great observed: "Learn of the Heart of God in the words of God, so that you may more ardently long for eternal things." (*Registr. epist, lib. IV ep. 31 ad Theodorum Medicum*: P.L. LXXVII, 706).

76. But the Heart of Christ was moved by an even greater charity when words full of love fell from His lips. Let Us cite some examples. When He saw the crowds tired and hungry, He exclaimed, "I have compassion on the crowd" *(Mk. 8,2)*. And when He gazed upon Jerusalem, his most beloved City, blinded by her sins and therefore destined for complete destruction, He said: "Jerusalem, Jerusalem! Thou who killest the prophets, and stonest those who are sent to thee! How often would I have gathered thy children together, as a hen gathers her young under her wings, but Thou wouldst not!" *(Mt. 23,37)*.

77. But, because of love for His Father and holy indignation, His Heart beat violently when He beheld the sacrilegious buying

and selling in the temple, and He rebuked the profaners of the temple with these words: "It is written, My house shall be called a house of prayer, but you have made it a den of thieves'" *(Mt. 21,13)*.

78. But His Heart was moved by a special love and fear when He saw that the hour of His most cruel sufferings was now at hand. He felt a natural repugnance for death and those sorrows which were rushing upon Him and cried out: "Father, if it is possible, let this cup pass away from me" *(Mt. 26, 39)*. But with love unconquered by the greatest grief when He received a kiss from the traitor, He addressed him with these words, which seem to be the last invitation of His Most Merciful Heart to a friend who was about to betray Him to His executioners with an impious, faithless and most hardened heart: "Friend, for what purpose hast thou come? Does thou betray the Son of Man with a kiss?" *(Mt. 26,50, Lk.22,48)*.

79. In truth, He spoke with exceedingly great love and pity when He said to the pious women weeping for Him as He was about to suffer the undeserved death of the Cross: "Daughters of Jerusalem, do not weep for me, but weep for yourselves and for your children ... for if in the case of green wood they do these things, what is to happen in the case of the dry?" *(Lk. 23,28,31)*.

80. And finally, our Divine Redeemer, hanging on the Cross felt His Heart on fire with varied and vehement affections, affections of the most ardent love, of dismay, of mercy, of a most intense longing, of serene calm, which affections are indeed most strikingly expressed by the following words: "Father, forgive them, for they do not know what they are doing" *(Lk.23,34)*. "My God, my God, why hast Thou forsaken Me?" *(Mt. 27,46)*. "Amen I say to thee, this day thou shalt be with Me in Paradise" *(Lk. 23,43)*. "I thirst" *(Jn.19,28)*. "Father, into Thy hands I commend My spirit" *(Lk. 23,46)*.

81. Who in truth could describe in a worthy manner those beatings of the Divine Heart, the indications of His infinite love,

when He bestowed His greatest gifts on man, that is, Himself in the sacrament of the Eucharist, His Most Holy Mother and the priestly office communicated to us?

82. Even before He ate the Last Supper with His disciples when He knew that He was going to institute the sacrament of His Body and Blood by the shedding of which the new covenant was to be consecrated, He felt His heart stirred by strong emotions, which He made known to the Apostles in these words: "I have greatly desired to eat this passover with you before I suffer" *(Lk. 22,15)*. These same emotions were even stronger, without doubt, when "having taken bread, He gave thanks and broke it and gave it to them saying 'This is My Body which is being given for you; do this in remembrance of me.' In like manner, he took also the cup after the supper, saying: 'This cup is the new covenant in my blood, which shall be shed for you' *(Lk.22, 19-20)*.

83. Rightly, therefore, one may affirm that the Divine Eucharist, both as a sacrament and as a sacrifice—the one He bestowed on men, the other He Himself continually offers "from the rising of the sun even to the going down" *(Mal., 1,11)*—and the priesthood are all really the gifts of the Most Sacred Heart of Jesus.

84. Indeed another most precious gift of His Most Sacred Heart is, as We have said, Mary, the sweet Mother of God and the most loving Mother of us all. For she was the Mother of Our Redeemer according to the flesh and His associate in recalling the children of Eve to the life of divine grace. And so she is rightly hailed as the spiritual Mother of Mankind. Wherefore St. Augustine, in writing of her says:

85. "Indeed she is the Mother of the members of the Saviour, which we are because she cooperated by love so that the faithful who are the members of that head might be born in the Church." *(De Sancta Virginitate*, VI, P.L.XL, 339).

86. And to the unbloody gift of Himself, under the appearance of bread and wine, Our Savior, Jesus Christ, wished, as a special proof of His intimate and infinite love to add the bloody sacrifice of the Cross. Indeed, in His way of acting, He gave an example of that sublime charity which He set before His disciples as the highest measure of love: "Greater love than this no one has, that one lay down his life for his friends" *(Jn. 15.13)*.

87. Wherefore, the love of Jesus Christ, the Son of God, by the sacrifice of Golgotha, clearly and richly proves the love of God Himself: "In this we have come to know His love that He laid down his life for us; and we likewise ought to lay down our life for the brethren" *(Jn. 2,16)*.

88. And in fact Our Divine Redeemer was nailed to the Cross more by His love than by the force of the executioners. His voluntary holocaust is the supreme gift which He bestowed on each man according to the concise words of the Apostle: "Who loved me, and gave Himself up for me" *(Gal. 2,20)*.

89. Therefore, there can be no doubt that the Most Sacred Heart of Jesus, since it is most intimately the sharer of the life of the Incarnate Word, and since it was assumed as an instrument of the Divinity, no less than the other members of His human nature in accomplishing the works of divine grace and omnipotence (Cfr. S.Thom. Sum. Theol. III, q.19, a.I: Ed. Leon. tom. XI, 1903, p.329) is the true symbol of the boundless love by which Our Saviour, through the shedding of His blood, contracted a mystical marriage with the Church. "Through charity He suffered for the Church who was to be united to Him as His spouse." (Sum. Theol. Suppl. q.42, a.1, ad 3m: Ed. Leon. tom. XII, 1906, p.81).

90. Therefore, from the wounded heart of Our Redeemer, the Church, the dispenser of the blood of the Redeemer, was born. From this wounded Heart the grace of the sacraments, from which the children of the Church draw supernatural life, flowed most profusely, as we read in the sacred liturgy: "From the pierced Heart, the Church, joined to Christ, is born ... Who

pourest forth grace from Thy Heart." *(Hymn ad Vesp. Festi. SS mi cordis Iesu.)* By reason of this symbol, which was not, indeed, unknown even to the ancient Fathers of the Church and ecclesiastical writers, the Common Doctor, as if reechoing these same sentiments writes: "Water flowed from Christ's side to wash us: blood to redeem us. Wherefore blood belongs to the sacrament of the Eucharist, while water belongs to the sacrament of Baptism. Yet this latter sacrament derives its cleansing virtue from the power of Christ's blood." *(Sum. Theol.*III, q.66, a.3, ad 3m; Ed. Leon. tom. XII, 1906, p.65).

91. What is written here concerning the side of Christ, wounded and opened by a soldier, must likewise be said of His Heart, which the lance actually touched with its stroke, inasmuch as the soldier pierced it so that he might be clearly certain of the death of Jesus Christ fixed to the Cross.

92. Wherefore the wound of the Most Sacred Heart of Jesus, which had now completed the course of this mortal life, is down through the ages the living image of that love freely bestowed by which God gave His only begotten Son for the redemption of Man, and with which Christ loved us all so intensely that He offered Himself for us as a bloody victim on Calvary: "Christ also loved us and delivered Himself up for us as an offering and a sacrifice to God to ascend in fragrant odor" *(Eph. 5,2)*.

93. After Our Saviour ascended into Heaven, with His body adorned with the splendor of eternal glory, and sat at the right hand of the father, His Heart beat with the most ardent love and He did not cease to manifest His love for His spouse, the Church. Indeed in His hands and feet and side He bears in majesty the glowing marks of the wounds which represent the triple victory gained by Him over the devil, sin and death.

94. He likewise has in His Heart, placed, as it were, in a most precious shrine, that treasure of merit, the fruit of His triple triumph. These He bestows generously on redeemed mankind. This is a truth full of consolation, which the Apostle of the

Gentiles stated in these words: "Ascending on high, He led away captives; he gave gifts to men. He who descended, He it is who ascended also above all the heavens, that He might fill all things." *(Eph.4, 8, 10)*.

95. The gift of the Holy Spirit to His disciples is the first clear sign of His munificent charity after His triumphal ascent to the right hand of the Father. Indeed after ten days the Spirit, the Paraclete, given by the Heavenly Father, descended upon them gathered in the Cenacle, as He had promised them at the Last Supper: I will ask the Father and He will give you another Advocate to dwell with you forever" *(Jn. 14, 16)*.

96. This Spirit, the Paraclete, since He is the personified mutual love of the Father for the Son and of the Son for the Father, is sent indeed by both. Assuming the appearance of tongues of fire, He poured the abundance of divine love and other heavenly gifts into their souls. The infusion of this divine love also sprang from the Heart of our Saviour "in whom are hidden all the treasures of wisdom and knowledge" *(Col.2,3)*.

97. Indeed, this love is the gift of the Heart of Jesus and His Spirit, who is indeed the Spirit of the Father and the Son and from whom both the rise of the Church and its remarkable spread is unfolded for all the pagan nations which the worship of idols, hatred of brothers, and corruption of morals as well as violence had befouled.

98. This divine love is the most precious gift of the Heart of Christ and of His Spirit. This love gave the apostles and martyrs that fortitude with which they were strengthened to fight even to the point of death, which they met with heroic spirit, to preach the truth of the gospel and to testify to it with their blood. This love gave to the Doctors of the Church a most ardent desire to teach and defend the Catholic Faith.

99. It was this love which nourished the virtues of the confessors and urged them to accomplish eminently useful and

marvelous deeds, profitable for their own eternal and temporal welfare and that of others. This was the love which persuaded virgins to abstain, willingly and joyfully, from sensual pleasures, and to consecrate themselves entirely to the love of their heavenly Spouse. This love, pouring forth from the Heart of the Incarnate Word, is infused by the Holy Spirit into the souls of all the faithful.

100. It brought forth that hymn of victory for the Apostle of the Gentiles, who proclaimed the triumph of the members of the Mystical Body and of Jesus Christ, its Head, and the restoration of the divine kingdom of love among men, no matter how they might try to prevent it: "Who shall separate us from the love of Christ? Shall tribulation, or distress, or persecution, or hunger, or nakedness, or danger, or the sword? But in all these things we overcome because of him who has loved us. For I am sure that neither death, nor life, nor angels, nor principalities, nor things present, nor things to come, nor powers, nor height, nor depth, nor any other creature will be able to separate us from the love of God which is in Christ Jesus our Lord." *(Rom. 8,35,37-39)*.

101. There is nothing, then, which forbids us to adore the Most Sacred Heart of Jesus, since it participates in and is the natural and most expressive symbol of that inexhaustible love with which Our Divine Redeemer still loves mankind. That heart indeed, even if it is no longer liable to the disturbances of this mortal life, still lives and beats. It is now inseparably joined with the Person of the Divine Word, and in it and through it with His divine will.

102. Wherefore, since the Heart of Christ overflows with divine and human love, and since it is abundantly rich with treasures of all graces which Our Redeemer acquired by His life and His sufferings, it is truly the unfailing fountain of that love which His Spirit pours forth into all the members of His Mystical Body.

103. Therefore the Heart of Our Saviour to some degree expresses the image of the Divine Person of the Word and His two-fold nature, human and divine. In it we can contemplate not only the symbol, but also, as it were, the sum of the whole mystery of our redemption.

104. When we adore the Most Sacred Heart of Jesus Christ we adore in it and through it both the uncreated love of the Divine Word and His human love and all His other affections and virtues. This is so because both loves moved Our Redeemer to sacrifice Himself for us and for the whole Church, His Spouse. As the Apostle says: "Christ also loved the Church and delivered Himself up for her, that He might sanctify her, cleansing in the bath of water by means of the Word, in order that he might present to Himself the Church in all her glory, not having spot or wrinkle or any such thing, but that she might be holy and without blemish" *(Eph. 5,25-27).*

105. As Christ loved the Church with that triple love of which We have spoken, He still loves her most deeply. This love moves Him as Our Advocate (Cfr.1 Jn.2,1) to gain grace and mercy for us from the Father, "since he lives always to make intercession for them" *(Heb. 7,25).* The prayers which come forth from His inexhaustible love and which are directed to the Father are never interrupted. As "in the days of His earthly life" *(Heb. 5,7)* so now triumphant in heaven He beseeches the Father with no less efficacy.

106. He shows His living Heart to Him who "so loved the world that he gave His only-begotten Son, that those who believe in Him may not perish, but may have life everlasting" *(Jn.3,16).* His Heart is, as it were, wounded and burning with even greater love than when it was pierced at death by the lance of a Roman soldier. "Wherefore (Thy Heart) was wounded so that through the visible wound we might see the invisible wound of love." (St. Bonventure, *Opusa. X: Vitis mystica,* c. III, N.5; *Opera Omnia, Ad Clarus Aguas* (Quarachi) 1898, tom. VIII, p. 164; Cfr. S.Thom. *Sum. Theol.* III, 9.54, a.4; Ed. Leon. tom. XI, 1903, p.513).

107. It is then absolutely certain that the Heavenly Father "who has not spared even His own Son, but has delivered Him for us all" *(Rom. 8,32)* when He has been asked by so powerful an Advocate and with such ardent love, will never at any time, diminish the rich flow of divine graces to all men.

IV

108. It has been Our wish, venerable brothers, to explain to you and to the faithful the real nature of devotion to the most Sacred Heart of Jesus in the light of divine revelation, its chief source, and the graces which flow from it.

109. We think that Our statements, confirmed by the teaching of the Gospel, have made it clear that essentially this devotion is nothing else than devotion to the human and divine love of the Incarnate Word and to the love which the Heavenly Father and the Holy Ghost have for sinful men.

110. For, as the Angelic Doctor teaches, the first cause of man's redemption is the love of the August Trinity. This love pouring forth abundantly into the human will of Jesus Christ and His Adorable Heart, moved Him to shed His blood to redeem us from the captivity of sin. (Cfr. *Sum. Theol.,* 3,q.48, a.5; Ed. Leon. tom. 11,1903, p.467). "I have a baptism to be baptized with; and how distressed I am until it is accomplished!" *(Lk. 12,50)*.

111. We know, therefore, that the devotion whereby we pay homage to Jesus Christ's love for men through the august sign of the Wounded Heart of the Redeemer nailed to the Cross has never been entirely unknown to Christian piety. In more recent times, however, this devotion has become better known and wondrously spread throughout the Church, particularly after the Lord Himself privately revealed this divine mystery to some of His children, richly endowed with an abundance of heavenly graces, and chose them as the messengers and heralds of this devotion.

112. Indeed, there always have been souls especially dedicated to God, who imitating the example of holy Mother of God, the Apostles and the illustrious Fathers of the Church, have adored, thanked and loved Christ's most sacred human nature, especially the wounds inflicted on His body during His salutary Passion.

113. Furthermore, do not these very words, "My Lord and my God" *(Jn.20,28)*, spoken by the Apostle Thomas signifying a person changed from an unbeliever into a faithful follower, contain a clear profession of faith, adoration and love rising from the wounded humanity of the Lord to the majesty of the Divine Person?

114. But if men were always strongly moved by the wounded heart of the Redeemer to venerate the infinite love with which He loves the human race, since the words of the Prophet Zacharias applied by St. John the Evangelist to Christ on the Cross, "They shall look upon Him whom they have pierced" *(Jn. 19,37, Za. 12,10)*, were addressed to the faithful of all ages, we must nevertheless admit that only gradually and by degrees was the homage of special devotion paid to His Heart as the image of the human and divine love in the Incarnate Word.

115. If we wish to sketch the significant stages in the progress of this devotion through the years, there immediately comes to mind the names of some who have gained special renown in this respect and who are to be considered the standard-bearers of this devotion which gradually gained momentum privately in religious communities.

116. We mention, by way of example, the names of those who achieved special distinction in establishing and promoting devotion to the Most Sacred Heart of Jesus: St. Bonaventure, St. Albert the Great, St. Gertrude, St. Catherine of Siena, Blessed Henry Suso, St. Peter Canisius, St. Francis de Sales and St. John Eudes, author of the first liturgical office to be celebrated in honor of the Most Sacred Heart of Jesus.

117. With the approval of many bishops of France, this solemn feast was celebrated for the first time on October 20, 1672.

118. Among those who have promoted this most excellent devotion, St. Margaret Mary Alacoque occupies the chief place of honor. Inflamed with great zeal and with the aid of her spiritual director, Blessed Claude de la Colombière, she succeeded in her efforts, not without the great admiration of the faithful, to have this devotion rich in spiritual blessings established and clearly distinguished from other forms of Christian piety by the special nature of its acts of love and reparation. (cfr. *Encycl. Miserentissimus Redemptor*: A.A.S., 20,1928, pp.167-168).

119. A review of the history of the period in which this devotion to the Most Sacred Heart of Jesus began is enough to increase our clear understanding that its marvelous progress is due to the fact that this devotion is in perfect accord with the nature of the Christian religion, which is indeed a religion of love.

120. Therefore, we must not say that this devotion began because it was privately revealed by God or that it suddenly came into existence in the Church, but that it is the spontaneous flowering of a living and fervent faith by which men filled with supernatural grace were led to adore the Redeemer and His glorious wounds as symbols of His boundless love which stirred their souls to the very depths.

121. Consequently, as is obvious, the revelations made to St. Margaret Mary added nothing new to Catholic doctrine. The significance of these revelations lies in this, that Christ the Lord—showing His Most Sacred Heart—willed in an extraordinary and special way to call the minds of men to the contemplation and veneration of the mystery of God's most merciful love for the human race.

122. And so in this special manifestation, in repeated and clear words, Christ pointed to His Heart as the symbol by which men are drawn to recognize and acknowledge His love, and at the same time constituted it as a sign and pledge of His mercy and His grace for the needs of the Church in our time.

123. Moreover, the fact that this devotion stems from the principles of Christian doctrine is clearly demonstrated by the fact that the Apostolic See approved the liturgical feast before it approved the writings of St. Margaret Mary. For, paying no specific attention to any private divine revelation, but graciously granting the petitions of the faithful, the Sacred Congregation of Rites in a decree of January 25, 1765, approved by Our predecessor, Clement XIII, on February 6 of the same year, granted the celebration of a liturgical feast to the Bishops of Poland and to the Roman Archfraternity of the Sacred Heart.

124. The Apostolic See granted this petition to extend an already existing and flourishing devotion whose purpose was "symbolically to renew the memory of that divine love" (Cfr. A. Gardellini, *Decreta Authentica*, 1857, N. 4579, tom. 3, P.174), by which our redeemer was impelled to offer Himself as a propitiary victim for the sins of men.

125. This first approbation was granted in the form of a privilege and was restricted to definite regions. After almost a century, another approbation followed of far greater importance, and phrased in more solemn words. We are referring, as We previously mentioned, to the decree of the Sacred Congregation of Rites issued August 23, 1856. By it Our predecessor of immortal memory Pius IX, acceding to the petitions of the Bishops of France and of almost the whole Catholic world ordered the feast of the Most Sacred Heart of Jesus to be extended to the entire Church and to be duly celebrated. (cfr. Decr. S.C. Rit. Apud. N. Nilles *De rationibus festorum Sacratissimi Cordis Jesu et purissimi Cordis Mariae*, 5th edition. Insbruek, 1995, tom. 1, p. 167). The faithful should always remember this decree, for, as we read in the liturgy of this feast,

"Since that time devotion to the Most Sacred Heart, gushing forth like a mighty stream, has spread throughout the world, washing away every obstruction in its course"

126. From the explanations which We have given, venerable brothers, it is perfectly clear that the faithful must trace devotion to the Most Sacred Heart of Jesus back to Sacred Scripture, tradition and the liturgy, if they wish to understand its real meaning and through pious meditation, receive food to nourish and increase their religious fervor.

127. If this devotion is constantly practiced with this knowledge and understanding, the souls of the faithful cannot but attain to the sweet knowledge of the love of Christ which is the acme of Christian life as the Apostle, who knew this from personal experience, teaches: "For this reason I bend my knees to the Father of our Lord Jesus Christ ... that he may grant you from His glorious riches to be strengthened with power through his Spirit unto the progress of the inner man; and to have Christ dwelling through faith in your hearts: so that, being rooted and grounded in love ... you know Christ's love which surpasses knowledge, in order that you may be filled unto all the fullness of God" *(Eph. 3,14,16-19)*.

128. The heart of Christ is the clearest image of this fullness of God embracing all things. By this We mean the fullness of mercy, which is the special characteristic of the New Testament in which "the goodness and kindness of God our Saviour appeared" *(Ti.3,4)*. "For God did not send his Son into the world in order to judge the world, but that the world might be saved through him" *(Jn.3,17)*.

129. From the very day in which she issued the first decree concerning devotion to the Most Sacred Heart of Jesus, the Church, the teacher of mankind, has always been certain that the essential characteristic of this devotion—that is acts of love and reparation by which God's infinite love for mankind is

venerated—is in no way infected with the poison of materialism or superstition.

130. On the contrary, this devotion is a form of piety by which the soul clearly discharges religious obligations and a perfectly true worship which the Saviour Himself foretold in His conversation with the Samaritan woman: "But the hour is coming, and is now here, when the true worshippers will worship the Father in spirit and in truth. For the Father also seeks such to worship him. God is spirit, and they who worship him must worship in spirit and in truth" *(Jn.4,23-24)*.

131. It is therefore wrong to say that the contemplation of the physical heart of Jesus is a hindrance to attaining intimate love of God, and that it impedes the soul in its progress to the highest virtues.

132. The Church completely condemns this false mysticism, just as she did when she spoke through Our predecessor of happy memory, Innocent XI, who condemned the errors of those who idly maintained: "Nor must they (souls of the interior way) elicit acts of love for the Blessed Virgin, or the saints or the humanity of Christ for, since these are sensible objects love for them is of the same nature. No creature, neither the Blessed Virgin nor the saints, must have a place in our heart; because God wishes to occupy and possess it." (Innocent XI, Constit.Ap. *Colelestis Pastor*, November 19, 1687; *Bullarium Romanum*, Rome, 1734, tom. 8, p 443.)

133. It is evident that those who hold such opinions think that the image of the Heart of Christ represents nothing nobler than His sensible love and that this image is not of such a nature as to be a new basis for adoration, which is given only to that which is by its nature divine.

134. There is no one who does not see that this interpretation of sacred images is entirely false. It confines their meaning, which is much broader, within too narrow limits. Catholic theologians, among them St. Thomas, write: "The worship of

religion is paid to images not as considered in themselves, nor as things, but as images leading us to God Incarnate. Now, movement to an image as image does not stop at the image, but goes on to the thing it represents. Hence, neither latria nor the virtue of religion is differentiated by the fact that. religious worship is paid to the images of Christ." *(Sum. Theol.*II-II,q.81 a.3 ad 3m; Ed. Leon. tom. 9, 1897, p.180).

135. The veneration paid to images, whose excellence must be determined by what is venerated, or to relics of the bitter sufferings which Our Saviour endured for us or to the picture of the pierced heart of Christ hanging on the Cross, which surpasses everything in force and meaning, is paid to the very person of the Incarnate Word as its final object.

136. Therefore, from the physical thing which the heart of Christ is, and from its natural signification, we can and must, supported by Christian faith, rise not only to contemplate His love, which is perceived through the senses, but even to meditate on and adore the most sublime infused love and finally the divine love of the Incarnate Word.

137. By faith, through which we believe that the human and the divine nature were united in the Person of Christ, we can see the closest bonds between the sensible love of the physical heart of Jesus and the two-fold spiritual love namely, human and divine.

138. We must not only say that these two loves were simultaneously present in the adorable Person of the Divine Redeemer, but also that they were joined by a natural bond so that the human and sensible loves are subject to the divine and bear its analogical resemblance. We do not, however, maintain that the Heart of Jesus is to be understood in such a way that in it we have and adore a formal image, as they say, or a perfect and absolute sign of His divine love, since the essence of this love can in no way be adequately expressed by any created image whatsoever.

139. But the Christian, in honoring the Heart of Jesus together with the Church, adores the sign and manifestation of divine love which went so far as to love through the heart of the Incarnate Word the human race defiled with countless sins.

140. It is therefore necessary, at this central point of a teaching which is so important and profound, that everyone bear in mind that the truth of the natural symbol by which the physical heart of Jesus is referred to the Person of the Word, rests completely on the fundamental doctrine of the hypostatic union.

141. Whoever denies that this doctrine is true would renew false teachings, repeatedly condemned by the Church, which deny that there is one Person in Christ with two distinct and complete natures.

142. With this fundamental truth firmly established, we understand that the heart of Jesus is the heart of a Divine Person, that is of the Incarnate Word, and that by it all the love with which He loved, and even now continues to love us is represented and, so to speak, placed before our very eyes.

143. Therefore, devotion to the Most Sacred Heart is so important that it may be considered, so far as practice is concerned, the perfect profession of the Christian religion.

144. For this is the religion of Jesus which rests entirely on a Mediator who is man and God, so that no one can come to the heart of God except through the heart of Christ as He Himself says: "I am the way, and the truth, and the life. No one comes to the father but through me" *(Jn. 14,6)*.

145. Since this is true, we readily understand that devotion to the Most Sacred Heart of Jesus is essentially devotion to the love with which God loved us through Jesus and is at the same time an enlivening of our love for God and man. Or, to put it in other

words, this devotion is directed to God's love for us in order to adore Him, to thank Him and to spend our lives imitating Him.

146. It seeks to lead us, in attaining this goal, to a strengthening of the bonds of love, with which we are bound to God and our fellow men, by daily observing more eagerly the new commandment which the Divine Master gave to His disciples as a sacred inheritance when He said; "A new commandment I give you, that you love one another: as I have loved you ... This is my commandment, that you love one another as I have loved you" *(Jn. 13,34; 15,12).*

147. This commandment is indeed new and Christ's very own. As St. Thomas says, "The difference between the Old and New Testaments is told in a few words, for as Jeremias says, 'I will make a new covenant with the house of Israel' *(Jer. 31,31).* However, because the commandment was in the Old Testament through fear and holy love, it related to the New Testament: hence this commandment was in the old law not as something that belonged to it but as a preparation for the new law." *(Comment. in Evang.* S. Joann. c.13, lect.7,3,ed. Parmae, 1860, tom. 10, p.541).

V

148. We have presented for your consideration the real nature and excellence of this devotion—beautiful teachings filled with consolation. But before We close this letter, mindful of Our apostolic office, which was first entrusted to St. Peter after his three-fold protestation of love for Christ the Lord, We deem it fitting to exhort you again, venerable brothers, and through you all of Our dearly beloved children in Christ, to strive ever more earnestly to promote this most gratifying devotion.

149. We are confident that in Our day, as in others, a great many blessings will flow from it.

150. Indeed, if the evidence on which devotion to the Wounded Heart of Jesus rests is rightly weighed, it is clear to all that we are dealing here, not with an ordinary form of piety

which anyone may at his discretion slight in favor of other devotions, or esteem lightly, but with a duty of religion most conducive to Christian perfection.

151. For if devotion, according to the common theological definition which the Angelic Doctor gives, "is apparently nothing else but the will to give oneself readily to things concerning the service of God" *(Sum. Theol.* II-II q. 82 a.I), can there be a service to God more required and necessary—and at the same time nobler and more pleasant—that which pays homage to His love?

152. What is more pleasing and acceptable to God than that service which submits to divine love and is rendered for the sake of love?

153. For every service freely rendered is in a sense a gift, and love "has the nature of a first gift in strength whereof all free gifts are given." *(Sum. Theol.* I.q.38 a.2).

154. That form of religion must be held in highest honor by which man honors and loves God more and more easily, and by which he more readily consecrates himself to divine love, which Our Redeemer Himself deigned to propose and recommend to Christianity and which the Sovereign Pontiffs have defended in their writings and extolled with highest praise.

155. Therefore, whoever considers of little value this outstanding gift of Jesus Christ to His Church, does a rash and harmful thing and offends God Himself.

156. There is, then, no doubt that the faithful, in honoring the Most Sacred Heart of the Redeemer, fulfill a more serious obligation by which they are bound to serve God and dedicate themselves and all they have, including their most secret thoughts and actions, to their Creator and Redeemer, and in this way obey the divine commandment: "Thou shalt love the Lord thy God with thy whole heart, and with thy whole soul, and with

thy whole mind, and with thy whole strength" *(Mk. 12,30; Mt. 22,37)*.

157. The faithful know with certainty that they are primarily led to worship God not for their own spiritual or physical, temporal or eternal advantage, but on account of the goodness of God, whom they seek to serve by loving Him in return, by adoring Him and thanking Him.

158. If this were not true, devotion to the Sacred Heart of Jesus would not be in accord with the true nature of the Christian religion, since by such devotion divine love is not primarily venerated. And, so those who incorrectly understand the nature of this devotion and practice it in the wrong way, are not unjustly, as sometimes happens, accused of excessive love and concern for themselves.

159. Let all therefore be firmly convinced that in showing devotion to the Most August Heart of Jesus, external acts of piety do not play the first and foremost role.

160. The reason for this devotion is not primarily to be sought in the blessings which Christ the Lord promised in private revelations. Rather it is that men should fulfill more fervently the principal duties of the Catholic faith, namely the obligations of love and expiation, and so also contribute greatly to their own spiritual advancement.

161. We therefore urge all Our sons in Christ eagerly to cherish this devotion, both those who already are accustomed to draw salutary waters from the heart of the Redeemer, and especially those who, in the idle manner of spectators, look on from a distance with misgivings.

162. Let them seriously consider that we speak of a devotion, as We have already said, which has long been firmly based on the Gospel and which tradition and the sacred liturgy openly encourage.

163. The Roman pontiffs themselves praised it most highly on numerous occasions, and were not content merely to institute a feast in honor of the Sacred Heart and extend it to the universal Church, but also solemnly consecrated and dedicated the whole human race to the Most Sacred Heart. (cfr. Leo XIII encycl. *Annum Sacrum* : A.Ls., vol.19, 1900, p.71 sq.; *Decr. S.C. Rituum* June 28,1899, in Decr, Auth. 3, x. 3712; Pius XI, encycl. *Miserentissimus Redemptor*: A.A. S. 1928, p.177sq.; *Decr. S.C. Rit.* January 29, 1929; A.A.S. 21, 1929, p.77).

164. Finally, We add the rich and most pleasing fruits of this devotion for the Church; the return of countless souls to the religion of Christ, the reanimated faith of many people and the closer union of the faithful with our most loving Redeemer, all of which, especially in these past few decades, have happened before Our eyes in ever increasing and richer profusion.

165. As we look upon this marvelous spectacle of devotion to the Most Sacred Heart of Jesus so widely spread and so ardent among all classes of the faithful, We are filled with joyous sentiments of gratitude.

166. After rendering fitting thanks to Our Redeemer, who is the infinite treasure of goodness, We cannot refrain from extending Our paternal congratulations to all, both of the clergy and of the laity, who have actively contributed to the spreading of this devotion.

167. Although devotion to the Most Sacred Heart of Jesus has everywhere produced the salutary fruits of Christian living, everyone knows, venerable brothers, that the Church Militant here on earth, and especially civil society, have not yet achieved that full and complete measure of perfection which corresponds to the wishes and desires of Jesus Christ, the Mystical Spouse of the Church and the Redeemer of the human race.

168. Not a few of the Church's children mar the beauty of their mother's countenance, which they reflect in themselves with too many blemishes and wrinkles. Not all the faithful are

resplendent with that sanctity of life to which they have been called by God.

169. All sinners have not returned to the Father's house, which they left through sin, there to put on once more the "best robe" *(Lk.15,22)*, and to receive for their finger a ring, the sign of fidelity to the Spouse of their soul.

170. Not all of the pagans, not even a goodly number, have yet been joined to the Mystical Body of Christ. For if the languishing faith of the good, in whose souls, led astray by the deceptive desire for worldly possession, the fervor of charity grows cold and is gradually extinguished, causes Us bitter grief, the machinations of the wicked wrack Us with even greater pain.

171. As if goaded on by the infernal enemy, these men, especially now, are on fire with an implacable and open hatred for God, the Church and especially for him who takes the place of the Divine Redeemer on earth and represents His love for men according to the memorable words of St. Ambrose: "For (Peter) is questioned in a matter about which he feels uncertain; but the Lord who put the question has no doubt. He asked not to find out, but to appoint before His ascension Him whom He left us as the Vicar of His love." *(Exposit. in Evang. sec. Lucam*, I, 10, n.175; P.L.15, 1942).

172. Indeed hatred of God and those who lawfully take His place is so great a sin that man, created in the image and likeness of God and destined to enjoy His friendship which is to last forever in heaven, can commit none greater.

173. By hatred of God, man is separated completely from the highest good and driven to cast from himself and his fellow men whatever comes from God, whatever joins us to God and whatever leads us to enjoy God, that is to reject truth, virtue, peace and justice. (Cfr. St. Thomas *Sum. Theol.* II-II, q 34, a.2; Ed. Leon. tom. 8, 1895, p. 274)

174. Unfortunately, since it is possible to see increasing everywhere the number of those who glory in being enemies of God, the false tenets of materialism being propagated in practice and theory, unbridled freedom of lust everywhere extolled, what wonder if charity—the supreme law of the Christian religion, the surest foundation of true and perfect justice, the chief source of peace and chaste pleasure—grow cold in the souls of many? For, as Our Saviour warned, "because iniquity will abound, the charity of the many will grow cold" *(Mt.24,12)*.

175. Faced with so many evils which today more than ever deeply disturb individuals, homes, nations and the whole world, where, venerable brothers, is a remedy to be found?

176. Is there a devotion more excellent that to the Most Sacred Heart of Jesus, one which is more in accord with the real nature of the Catholic faith or which better meets the needs of the Church and the human race today? What act of religion is nobler, more suitable, sweeter and more conducive to salvation, since this devotion is wholly directed to the love of God Himself? (cfr. Encycl. *Miserentissimus Redemptor*: A.A.S. 20, 1928, p. 166).

177. Finally, what is more powerful than the love of Christ which devotion to the Most Sacred Heart daily increases and fosters?

178. This love can truly bring the faithful to live the law of the Gospel.

179. If this law is rejected, is it possible to have genuine peace among men? For as the words of the Holy Ghost clearly teach, "The work of justice shall be peace" *(Is. 32,17)*.

180. Therefore, following the example of Our immediate predecessor, We choose to address again all Our beloved sons in Christ in the words of admonition which Leo XIII of immortal memory spoke to all the faithful at the end of the last century.

181. We likewise address these words to all who have a genuine concern for their own salvation and that of civil society. "Behold another most auspicious and divine standard presented to our view today: the Most Sacred Heart of Jesus gleaming with dazzling light surrounded by flames. In it all hopes must be placed, in it man's salvation must be sought and looked for." (Encycl. *Annum Sacrum*: A.L. vol. 19, 1900, p.79; *Miserentissimus Redemptor*; A.A.S., 20, 1928, p.167).

182. It is also Our most ardent desire that all who glory in the name of Christian and who zealously strive to establish the Kingdom of Christ in earth, consider devotion to the Heart of Jesus as the standard and the source of unity, salvation and peace.

183. Nevertheless, let no one think that this devotion detracts anything from other devotions with which Christian people, under the leadership of the Church, honor the Divine Redeemer.

184. On the contrary, ardent devotion to the Heart of Jesus will without doubt encourage and promote devotion to the Most Holy Cross and love for the Most August Sacrament of the Altar. For We can definitely state a fact which the revelations made by Jesus Christ to St. Gertrude and St. Margaret marvelously confirm: that no one ever fittingly loves Christ hanging on the Cross but he to whom the mystical secrets of His Sacred Heart have been unfolded.

185. Not will it be easy to grasp the force of that love by which Christ was impelled to give us himself as our spiritual food except by fostering a special devotion to the Eucharistic Heart of Jesus.

186. The purpose of this devotion, to use the words of Our predecessor of happy memory, Leo XIII, is to recall to our minds "that supreme act of love by which Our Redeemer, pouring forth all the riches of His Heart, instituted the adorable sacrament of the Eucharist to remain in our midst to the end of time." (*Litt. Apost.*

Quibus Archisodalitas a Corde Eucharistico Jesu ad S. Jochim de Urbe erigitur, February 17, 1903; A.L. Vol. 22,1903, p.307 sq.; cfr. Encycl. *Mirae caritatis*, May 22, 1902: A.L. Vol. 22, 1903, p.116).

187. For "the Eucharist is not the smallest portion of His Heart which He gave us from the overflowing loving of His heart." (St. Albert the Great, *De Eucharistia*, dist. 6, tr. I, C.I: *Opera Omnia*; Ed. Borgnet, Vol. 38, Paris 1890, P. 358).

188. Finally, greatly impelled by the desire to set up a firm defence against the wicked machinations of the enemies of God and His Church, and at the same time to lead back domestic and civil society to the love of God and neighbor, We do not hesitate to state emphatically that devotion to the Sacred Heart of Jesus is the most effective school of divine charity, on which the Kingdom of God to be established in the souls of individuals, in families and in nations must rest.

189. As Our same predecessor of blessed memory most wisely teaches: "The kingdom of Jesus Christ draws its power and distinctive characteristic from divine love; its foundation and chief doctrine is to love holily and in proper order. From this it necessarily follows that we must fulfill obligations faithfully, not infringe on the rights of others, consider human matters inferior to divine and place love of God above everything else." (Encycl. *Tametsi*, A.L. Vol. 20, 1900, p.303.)

190. That graces for the Christian family and for the whole human race may flow more abundantly from devotion to the Sacred Heart, let the faithful strive to join it closely with devotion to the Immaculate Heart of the Mother of God.

191. By the will of God, the Most Blessed Virgin Mary was inseparately joined with Christ in accomplishing the work of man's redemption, so that our salvation flows from the love of Jesus Christ and His sufferings, intimately united with the love and sorrows of His mother.

192. It is, then, highly fitting that after due homage has been paid to the Most Sacred Heart of Jesus, Christian people who have obtained divine life from Christ through Mary, manifest similar piety and the love of their grateful souls for the most loving heart of our heavenly Mother.

193. The memorable act of consecration by which We Ourselves, in the wise and loving dispositions of Divine Providence, solemnly dedicated the Church and the whole world to the Immaculate Heart of the Blessed Virgin Mary, is in perfect accord with devotion to the Sacred Heart. (cfr. A.A.S. 34, 1942, P. 345).

194. Since in the course of the present year, as previously mentioned, We are joyfully completing the first century since Our predecessor of happy memory, Pius IX, ordered the celebration of the feast of the Most Sacred Heart of Jesus throughout the entire Church, it is Our fervent desire, venerable brothers, that this centenary be solemnly celebrated by the faithful everywhere with public acts of adoration, thanksgiving and reparation to the Divine Heart of Jesus.

195. With all the faithful united in bonds of love and common prayer, these festivals of Christian joy and piety will be celebrated with special religious fervor in that country where by God's special providence St. Margaret Mary, the promoter and indefatigable herald of this devotion, was born.

196. In the meantime, strengthened with new hope and in spirit already gathering the spiritual fruits which We are certain will grow abundantly in the Church from devotion to the Sacred Heart, if correctly understood according to Our explanation and zealously practiced, We humbly pray God lovingly to grant His grace for the fulfillment of Our most ardent desire.

197. With God's help may this year's celebration increase from day to day the love of the faithful for the Most Sacred Heart of Jesus. And may His kingdom, "a kingdom of truth and life, a kingdom of holiness and grace, a kingdom of justice, love

and peace" (Roman Missal *Preface of Jesus Christ the King*), be extended further to all in the whole world.

198. As a pledge of these heavenly graces, We most lovingly impart to each of you, venerable brothers, to the clergy and people entrusted to your care, and in particular those who zealously encourage and promote devotion to the Most Sacred Heart of Jesus, Our apostolic benediction.

199. Given at Rome from St. Peter's, May 15, 1956, in the eighteenth year of Our pontificate.

Translation: National Catholic Welfare Conference News Service.

OCTOBRI MENSE

ENCYCLICAL OF POPE LEO XIII
ON THE ROSARY
SEPTEMBER 22, 1891

To our Venerable Brethren the Patriarchs, Primates, Archbishops, and other Ordinaries having Grace and communion with the Apostolic See.

Venerable Brethren, Greeting and Apostolic Benediction.

At the coming of the month of October, dedicated and consecrated as it is to the Blessed Virgin of the Rosary, we recall with satisfaction the instant exhortations which in preceding years We addressed to you, venerable brethren, desiring as We did, that the faithful, urged by your authority and by your zeal, should redouble their piety towards the august Mother of God, the mighty helper of Christians, and should pray to her throughout the month, invoking her by that most holy rite of the Rosary which the Church, especially in the passage of difficult times, has ever used for the accomplishment of all desires. This year once again do We publish Our wishes, once again do We encourage you by the same exhortations. We are persuaded to this in love for the Church, whose sufferings, far from mitigating, increase daily in number and in gravity. Universal and well-known are the evils we deplore: war made upon the sacred dogmas which the Church holds and transmits; derision cast upon the integrity of that Christian morality which she has in keeping; enmity declared, with the impudence of audacity and with criminal malice, against the very Christ, as though the Divine work of Redemption itself were to be destroyed from its foundation—that work which, indeed, no adverse power shall ever utterly abolish or destroy.

2. No new events are these in the career of the Church militant. Jesus foretold them to His disciples. That she may teach

men the truth and may guide them to eternal salvation, she must enter upon a daily war; and throughout the course of ages she has fought, even to martyrdom, rejoicing and glorifying herself in nothing more than in the occasion of signing her cause with her Founder's blood, the sure and certain pledge of the victory whereof she holds the promise. Nevertheless we must not conceal the profound sadness with which this necessity of constant war afflicts the righteous. It is indeed a cause of great sorrow that so many should be deterred and led astray by error and enmity to God; that so many should be indifferent to all forms of religion, and should finally become estranged from faith; that so many Catholics should be such in name only, and should pay to religion no honor or worship. And still sadder and more beset with anxieties grows the soul at the thought of the fruitful source of the most manifold evils existing in the organization of States that allow no place to the Church, and that oppose her championship of holy virtue. This is truly a terrible manifestation of the just vengeance of God, Who allows blindness of soul to darken upon the nations that forsake Him. These are evils that cry aloud, that cry of themselves with a daily increasing voice. It is absolutely necessary that the Catholic voice should also call to God with unwearied instance, "without ceasing" *(Thes. 5.17)*; that the Faithful should pray not only in their own homes, but in public, gathered together under the sacred roof; that they should beseech urgently the all-foreseeing God to deliver the Church from evil men *(2 Thes. 3.2)* and to bring back the troubled nations to good sense and reason, by the light and love of Christ.

3. Wonderful and beyond hope or belief is this. The world goes on its laborious way, proud of its riches, of its power, of its arms, of its genius; the Church goes onward along the course of ages with an even step, trusting in God only, to Whom, day and night, she lifts her eyes and her suppliant hands. Even though in her prudence she neglects not the human aid which Providence and the times afford her, not in these does she put her trust, which rests in prayer, in supplication, in the invocation of God. Thus it is that she renews her vital breath; the diligence of her

prayer has caused her, in her aloofness from worldly things and in her continual union with the Divine will, to live the tranquil and peaceful life of Our very Lord Jesus Christ; being herself the image of Christ, Whose happy and perpetual joy was hardly marred by the horror of the torments He endured for us. This important doctrine of Christian wisdom has been ever believed and practiced by Christians worthy of the name. Their prayers rise to God eagerly and more frequently when the cunning and the violence of the perverse afflict the Church and her supreme Pastors. Of this the faithful of the Church in the East gave an example that should be offered to the imitation of posterity. Peter, Vicar of Jesus Christ, and first Pontiff of the Church, had been cast into prison, loaded with chains by the guilty Herod, and left for certain death. None could carry him help or snatch him from the peril. But there was the certain help that fervent prayer wins from God. The Church, as the sacred story tells us, made prayer without ceasing to God for him *(Acts 12,5)*; and the greater was the fear of a misfortune, the greater was the fervor of all who prayed to God. After the granting of their desires the miracle stood revealed; and Christians still celebrate with a joyous gratitude the marvel of a deliverance of Peter. Christ has given us a still more memorable instance, a Divine instance, so that the Church might be formed not upon His precepts only, but upon His example also. During His whole Life He had given Himself to frequent and fervent prayer, and in the supreme hours in the Garden of Gethsemane, when His soul was filled with bitterness and sorrow unto death, He prayed to His Father and prayed repeatedly *(Lk. 22,44)*. It was not for Himself that He prayed thus, for He feared nothing and needed nothing, being God; He prayed for us, for His Church, whose prayers and future tears He already then accepted with joy, to give them back in mercies.

4. But since the salvation of our race was accomplished by the mystery of the Cross, and since the Church, dispenser of that salvation after the triumph of Christ, was founded upon earth and instituted, Providence established a new order for a new people. The consideration of the Divine counsels is united to the great

sentiment of religion. The Eternal Son of God, about to take upon Him our nature for the saving and ennobling of man, and about to consummate thus a mystical union between Himself and all mankind, did not accomplish His design without adding there the free consent of the elect Mother, who represented in some sort all human kind, according to the illustrious and just opinion of St. Thomas, who says that the Annunciation was effected with the consent of the Virgin standing in the place of humanity. (III.q.xxx,a.l). With equal truth may it be also affirmed that, by the will of God, Mary is the intermediary through whom is distributed unto us this immense treasure of mercies gathered by God, for mercy and truth were created by Jesus Christ *(Jn. 1,17)*. Thus as no man goeth to the Father but by the Son, so no man goeth to Christ but by His Mother. How great are the goodness and mercy revealed in this design of God! What a correspondence with the frailty of man! We believe in the infinite goodness of the Most High, and we rejoice in it; we believe also in His justice and we fear it. We adore the beloved Savior, lavish of His blood and of His life; we dread the inexorable Judge. Thus do those whose actions have disturbed their consciences need an intercessor mighty in favor with God, merciful enough not to reject the cause of the desperate, merciful enough to lift up again toward hope in the divine mercy the afflicted and the broken down. Mary is this glorious intermediary; she is the mighty Mother of the Almighty; but— what is still sweeter—she is gentle, extreme in tenderness, of a limitless loving-kindness. As such God gave her to us. Having chosen her for the Mother of His only begotten Son, He taught her all a mother's feeling that breathes nothing but pardon and love. Such Christ desired she should be, for He consented to be subject to Mary and to obey her as a son a mother. Such He proclaimed her from the cross when he entrusted to her care and love the whole of the race of man in the person of His disciple John. Such, finally, she proves herself by her courage in gathering in the heritage of the enormous labors of her Son, and in accepting the charge of her maternal duties towards us all.

5. The design of this most dear mercy, realized by God in Mary and confirmed by the testament of Christ, was comprehended at the beginning, and accepted with the utmost joy by the Holy Apostles and the earliest believers. It was the counsel and teaching of the venerable Fathers of the Church. All the nations of the Christian age received it with one mind; and even when literature and tradition are silent there is a voice that breaks from every Christian breast and speaks with all eloquence. No other reason is needed than that of a Divine faith which, by a powerful and most pleasant impulse, persuades us towards Mary. Nothing is more natural, nothing more desirable than to seek a refuge in the protection and in the loyalty of her to whom we may confess our designs and our actions, our innocence and our repentance, our torments and our joys, our prayers and our desires—all our affairs. All men, moreover, are filled with the hope and confidence that petitions which might be received with less favor from the lips of unworthy men, God will accept when they are recommended by the most Holy Mother, and will grant with all favors. The truth and the sweetness of these thoughts bring to the soul an unspeakable comfort; but they inspire all the more compassion for those who, being without Divine faith, honor not Mary and have her not for their mother; for those also who, holding Christian faith, dare to accuse of excess the devotion to Mary, thereby sorely wounding filial piety.

6. This storm of evils, in the midst of which the Church struggles so strenuously, reveals to all her pious children the holy duty whereto they are bound to pray to God with instance, in the manner in which they may give to their prayers the greater power. Faithful to the religious example of our fathers, let us have recourse to Mary, our holy Sovereign. Let us entreat, let us beseech, with one heart, Mary, the Mother of Jesus Christ, our Mother. "Show thyself to be a mother; cause our prayers to be accepted by Him Who, born for us, consented to be thy Son." (Ex. sacr. liturg.)

7. Now, among the several rites and manners of laying honor to the Blessed Mary, some are to be preferred, inasmuch as we know them to be most powerful and most pleasing to our Mother; and for this reason we specially mention by name and recommend the Rosary. The common language has given the name of *corona* to this manner of prayer, which recalls to our minds the great mysteries of Jesus and Mary united in joys, sorrows and triumphs. The contemplation of these august mysteries, contemplated in their order, affords to faithful souls a wonderful confirmation of faith, protection against the disease of error, and increase of the strength of the soul. The soul and memory of him who thus prays, enlightened by faith, are drawn towards these mysteries by the sweetest devotion, are absorbed therein and are surprised before the work of the Redemption of mankind, achieved at such a price and by events so great. The soul is filled with gratitude and love before these proofs of Divine love; its hope becomes enlarged and its desire is increased for those things which Christ has prepared for such as have united themselves to Him in imitation of His example and in participation in His sufferings. The prayer is composed of words proceeding from God Himself, from the Archangel Gabriel, and from the Church; full of praise and of high desires; and it is renewed and continued in an order at once fixed and various; its fruits are ever new and sweet.

8. Moreover, we may well believe that the Queen of Heaven herself has granted an especial efficacy to this mode of supplication, for it was by her command and counsel that the devotion was begun and spread abroad by the holy Patriarch Dominic as a most potent weapon against the enemies of the faith at an epoch not, indeed, unlike our own, of great danger to our holy religion. The heresy of the Albigenses had in effect, one while covertly, another while openly, overrun many countries, and this most vile offspring of the Manicheans, whose deadly errors it reproduced, were the cause in stirring up against the Church the most bitter animosity and a virulent persecution. There seemed to be no human hope of opposing this fanatical and most pernicious sect when timely succor came from on high

through the instrument of Mary's Rosary. Thus under the favor of the powerful Virgin, the glorious vanquisher of all heresies, the forces of the wicked were destroyed and dispersed, and faith issued forth unharmed and more shining than before. All manner of similar instances are widely recorded, and both ancient. and modern history furnish remarkable proofs of nations saved from perils and winning benedictions therefrom. There is another signal argument in favor of this devotion, inasmuch as from the very moment of its institution it was immediately encouraged and put into most frequent practice by all classes of society. In truth, the piety of the Christian people honors, by many titles and in multiform ways, the Divine Mother, who, alone most admirable among all creatures, shines resplendent in unspeakable glory. But this title of the Rosary, this mode of prayer which seems to contain, as it were, a final pledge of affection, and to sum up in itself the honor due to Our Lady, has always been highly cherished and widely used in private and in public, in homes and in families, in the meetings of confraternities, at the dedication of shrines, and in solemn processions; for there has seemed to be no better means of conducting sacred solemnities, or of obtaining protection and favors.

9. Nor may we permit to pass unnoticed the especial Providence of God displayed in this devotion; for through the lapse of time religious fervor has sometimes seemed to diminish in certain nations, and even this pious method of prayer has fallen into disuse; but piety and devotion have again flourished and become vigorous in a most marvelous manner, when, either through the grave situation of the commonwealth or through some pressing public necessity, general recourse has been had— more to this than to every other means of obtaining help—to the Rosary, whereby it has been restored to its place of honor on the altars. But there is no need to seek for examples of this power in a past age, since we have in the present a signal of it. In these times—so troublous (as we have said before) for the Church, and so heartrending for ourselves—set as We are by the Divine will at the helm, it is still given Us to note with admiration the great zeal and fervor with which Mary's Rosary is honored and recited

in every place and nation of the Catholic world. And this circumstance, which assuredly is to be attributed to the Divine action and direction upon men, rather than to the wisdom and efforts of individuals, strengthens and consoles Our heart, filling Us with great hope for the ultimate and most glorious triumph of the Church under the auspices of Mary.

10. But there are some who, whilst they honestly agree with what We have said, yet because their hopes—especially as regard the peace and tranquility of the Church—have not yet been fulfilled, nay, rather because troubles seem to augment, have ceased to pray with diligence and fervor, in a fit of discouragement. Let these look into themselves and labor that the prayers they address to God may be made in a proper spirit, according to the precept of our Lord Jesus Christ. And if there be such, let them reflect how unworthy and how wrong it is to wish to assign to Almighty God the time and the manner of giving His assistance, since He owes nothing to us, and when He hearkens to our supplications and crowns our merits, *He only crowns His own innumerable benefits* (S. August. *Epi CXCIV al 106 Sixtum*, C. Y., n.19.); and when he complies least with our wishes it is as a good father towards his children, having pity on their childishness and consulting their advantage. But as regards the prayers which we join to the suffrages of the heavenly citizens, and offer humbly to God to obtain His mercy for the Church, they are always favorably received and heard, and either obtain for the Church great and imperishable benefits, or their influence is temporarily withheld for a time of greater need. In truth, to these supplications is added an immense weight and grace—the prayers and merits of Christ Our Lord, Who *has loved the Church and has delivered Himself up for her to sanctify her... so that He should be glorified in her (Eph. 5,25-27)*. He is her Sovereign Head, holy innocent, always living to make intercession for us, on whose prayers and supplication we can always by divine authority rely. As for what concerns the exterior and temporal prosperity of the Church, it is evident that she has to cope with most malicious and powerful adversaries. Too often has she suffered at their hands the abolition of her

rights, the diminution and oppression of her liberties, scorn and
affronts to her authority, and every conceivable outrage. And if
in their wickedness her enemies have not accomplished all the
injury they had resolved upon and striven to do, they
nevertheless seem to go on unchecked. But, despite them the
Church, amidst all these conflicts, will always stand out and
increase in greatness and glory. Nor can human reason rightly
understand why evil, apparently so dominant, should yet be so
restricted as regards its results; while the Church, driven into
straits, comes forth glorious and triumphant. And she ever
remains more steadfast in virtue because she draws men to the
acquisition of the ultimate good. And since this is her mission,
her prayers must have much power to effect the end and purpose
of God's providential and merciful designs towards men. Thus,
when men pray with and through the Church, they at length
obtain what Almighty God has designed from all eternity to
bestow upon mankind. (S.Th.II-II,q LXXXIII,a.2, ex S.G. reg M). The
subtlety of the human intelligence fails now to grasp the high
designs of Providence; but the time will come when, through the
goodness of God, causes and effects will be made clear, and the
marvelous power and utility of prayer will be shown forth. Then
it will be seen how many in the midst of a corrupt age have kept
themselves pure and inviolate from all concupiscence of the
flesh and the spirit, working out their sanctification in the fear of
God *(2 Cor. 7,1)*; how others, when exposed to the danger of
temptation, have without delay restrained themselves, gaining
new strength for virtue from the peril itself; how others, having
fallen, have been seized with the ardent desire to be restored to
the embraces of a compassionate God. Therefore, with these
reflections before them, We beseech all again and again not to
yield to the deceits of the old enemy, nor for any cause
whatsoever to cease from the duty of prayer. Let their prayers be
persevering, let them pray without intermission; let their first
care be to supplicate for the sovereign good—the eternal
salvation of the whole world, and the safety of the Church. Then
they may ask from God other benefits for the use and comfort of
life, returning thanks always, whether their desires are granted or
refused, as to a most indulgent father. Finally, may they converse

with God with the greatest piety and devotion according to the example of the Saints, and that of our Most Holy Master and Redeemer, *with great cries and tears (Heb. 5,7)*.

11. Our fatherly solicitude urges Us to implore of God, the Giver of all good gifts, not merely the spirit of prayer, but also that of holy penance for all the sons of the Church. And while We make this most earnest supplication, We exhort all and each one to the practice with equal fervor of both these virtues combined. Thus prayer fortifies the soul, makes it strong for noble endeavors, leads it up to divine things: penance enables us to overcome ourselves, especially our bodies—most inveterate enemies of reason and the evangelical law. And it is very clear that these virtues unite well with each other, assist each other mutually, and have the same object, namely to detach man born for heaven from perishable objects, and to raise him up to heavenly commerce with God. On the other hand, the mind that is excited by passions and enervated by pleasure is insensible to the delights of heavenly things, and makes cold and neglectful prayers quite unworthy of being accepted by God. We have before Our eyes examples of the penance of holy men whose prayers and supplications were consequently most pleasing to God, and even obtained miracles. They governed and kept assiduously in subjection their minds and hearts and wills. They accepted with the greatest joy and humility the doctrines of Christ and the teachings of His Church. Their unique desire was to advance in the science of God; nor had their actions any other object than the increase of His Glory. They restrained most severely their passions, treated their bodies rudely and harshly, abstaining from even permitted pleasures through love of virtue. And therefore most deservedly could they have said with the Apostle Paul, *our conversation is in Heaven (Phil.3,20)*: hence the potent efficacy of their prayers in appeasing and in supplicating the Divine Majesty. It is clear that not everyone is obliged or able to attain to these heights; nevertheless, each one should correct his life and morals in his own measure in satisfaction to the Divine justice: for it is to those who have endured voluntary sufferings in this life that the reward of virtue

is vouchsafed. Moreover, when in the mystical body of Christ, which is the Church, all the members are united and flourish, it results, according to St. Paul, that the joy or pain of one member is shared by all the rest, so that if one of the brethren in Christ is suffering in mind or body the others come to his help and succor him as far as in them lies. The members are solicitous in regard of each other, and if one member suffer all the members suffer in sympathy, and if one member rejoice all the others rejoice also. But you are the body of Christ, members of one body *(1 Cor.12,25-27)*. But in this illustration of charity, following the example of Christ, Who in the immensity of His Love gave up His life to redeem us from sin, paying Himself the penalties incurred by others, in this is the great bond of perfection by which the faithful are closely united with the heavenly citizens and with God. Above all, acts of holy penance are so numerous and varied and extend over such a wide range, that each one may exercise them frequently with a cheerful and ready will without serious or painful effort.

12. And now, venerable brethren, your remarkable and exalted piety towards the Most Holy Mother of God, and your charity and solicitude for the Christian flock, are full of abundant promise: Our heart is full of desire for those wondrous fruits which, on many occasions, the devotion of Catholic people to Mary has brought forth; already we enjoy them deeply and abundantly in anticipation. At your exhortation and under your direction, therefore, the faithful, especially during this ensuing month, will assemble around the solemn altars of this august Queen and most benign Mother, and weave and offer to her, like devoted children, the mystic garland so pleasing to her of the Rosary. All the privileges and indulgences We have herein before conceded are confirmed and ratified. (Cf. ep. encycl. *Supremi Apostolatus Officio* [September 1, 1883]; ep. encycl. *Superiore anno* [August 30, 1884]; decree *S.R.C. Inter plurimos* [August 20, 1885]; ep. encycl. *Quamquam pluries* [August 15, 1889].

13. How grateful and magnificent a spectacle to see in the cities, and towns, and villages, on land and sea—wherever the

Catholic faith has penetrated—many hundreds of thousands of pious people uniting their praises and prayers with one voice and heart at every moment of the day, saluting Mary, invoking Mary, hoping everything through Mary. Through her may all the faithful strive to obtain from her Divine Son that the nations plunged in error may return to the Christian teaching and precepts, in which is the foundation of "the public safety and the source of peace and true happiness" Through her may they steadfastly endeavor for that most desirable of all blessings, the restoration of the liberty of our Mother, the Church, and the tranquil possession of her rights—rights which have no other object that the careful direction of men's dearest interests, from the exercise of which individuals and nations have never suffered injury, but have derived, in all time, numerous and most precious benefits.

14: And for you, venerable brethren, through the intercession of the Queen of the Most Holy Rosary, We pray Almighty God to grant you heavenly gifts, and greater and more abundant strength, and aid to accomplish the charge of your pastoral office. As a pledge of which We most lovingly bestow upon you and upon the clergy and people committed to your care, the Apostolic Benediction.

Given at Rome, St. Peter's, the 22nd day of September, 1891, in the fourteenth year of Our Pontificate.

English translation: _Tablet,_ *78, (October 10, 1891), 573-75.*

53313156R00095

Made in the USA
Charleston, SC
07 March 2016